WHAT
MATTERS
TO YOU?
MATTERS
TO US

what matters to you? matters to us

ENGAGING SIX VITAL THEMES OF OUR FAITH

SIDNEY D. FOWLER

UNITED CHURCH PRESS
CLEVELAND

I am especially grateful to David Schoen, Vivian Santiago-Riccio, Christina Villa, Ken Ostermiller, Charlene Smith, Sandy Sorenson, Susan Blain, Barbara Brown Zikmund, Carol Wehrheim, Timothy Staveteig, Janice Brown, Jeffrey Catts, and Hope UCC in Alexandria, VA. Blessings to the many UCC members and vital congregations who were interviewed and, by God's grace, are unafraid to ask and live the bold questions of faith. — SIDNEY D. FOWLER

United Church Press, 700 Prospect Avenue, Cleveland, Ohio 44115-1100
unitedchurchpress.com
© 2008 United Church Press

Scripture quotations, unless otherwise noted, are from the New Revised Standard Version of the Bible, © 1989 by the Division of Christian Education of the National Council of Churches of Christ in the United States of America and are used by permission. Changes have been made for inclusivity.

To obtain a free study guide, please look up this book on www.unitedchurchpress .com. Also available online or by calling 800-537-3394 are *What Matters to You?* brochures: Assorted covers (LCMCV1); "What Matters to You? Matters to Us" cover (LCMCV1E); "Find Yourself. We Have GPS" cover (LCMCV1A); "Our Faith is 2000 Years Old, Our Thinking Is Not" cover (LCMV1B); "Please Return" cover (LCMCV1C); "United Not Divided" cover (LCMCV1D); or a set of six posters, one for each theme (LCMCVIO).

Printed in the United States of America on acid-free paper that contains post-consumer fiber.

13   12   11   10   09   08   5   4   3   2   1

Library of Congress Cataloging-in-Publication Data

Fowler, Sidney D.
    What matters to you? matters to us : engaging six vital themes of our faith / Sidney D. Fowler.
        p. cm.
    Includes bibliographical references and index.
    ISBN 978-0-8298-1800-0 (alk. paper)
    1. United Church of Christ—Doctrines.   I. Title.
BX9886.F69 2008
285.8'34—dc22   2008019225

contents

special resources

Ask the questions that are deep in your heart or dance in your head.

Together, we'll listen for God who still speaks today.

introduction:
what matters to you?
live the questions now

Take a deep breath and wonder: What matters to you? How do you spend your life? What are your hopes, your doubts, and your questions? For what do you seem to pray about the most? These are engaging questions, questions of faith.

This resource links your questions with those of the larger community of the United Church of Christ (UCC). We have said in a popular ad, "No matter who you are or where you are on life's journey, you are welcome here—the United Church of Christ." Whether you are a curious inquirer or a long-term member of the UCC, your questions matter. God is in the questions.

So go ahead, ask the questions that are deep in your heart and dance in your head: What about God, about Jesus, about justice? What about issues that people and nations debate, sometimes violently? What about life, death, and beyond? What about creation and those with whom we share this planet? What about so many people from different religions and no religion? What about hope, faith, and, yes, love? What's God to do with us? And even, why did God give you breath and life?

The German poet Rainer Maria Rilke once responded to the questions from a beginning eager artist. His words to the young poet are fitting as well to us with our questions of faith: "I beg you . . . to have patience with everything unresolved in your heart and to try to love the questions themselves. . . . And the point is, to live everything. Live the questions now. Perhaps, then, someday in the future, you will gradually, without even noticing it, live your way into the answers."[1]

The United Church of Christ wants to love the questions with you. We want to live into the answers with you. The UCC has always been a people of the searching heart, the inquisitive mind, and a restless longing for justice and peace. Some churches find strength in demanding loyalty to unquestionable answers. We seek answers also, yet we don't avoid the questions.

Together, with you, we bring our inquiry to God and listen—listen for a God who still speaks today. We know that often—while prayerfully seeking God's way with others—answers do come. Then we take a risk, make a stand, and proclaim the good news of Christ. And even still, in each generation, we listen again for more from God, for more wisdom, more truth, and more light. You are a vital part of *this* generation's listening for God.

This book encourages you to explore your questions and engage in questions that the UCC has pondered through the years. Perhaps you've considered becoming part of a church, or wondered about baptism, or just want to go deeper in your faith; this resource may help you explore questions along your search. It engages you around six vital themes of our faith. Rather than a list of UCC beliefs, this resource describes who we are as much as what we believe. The themes begin with the words "We are . . ." At this point along your journey of faith, do the themes reflect the kind of community of faith that God is calling you to join?

The first six chapters introduce you to the themes. Read straight through the chapters or, better, slow down; take your time to prayerfully reflect or talk with others. Each chapter invites you to offer your own questions and to reflect on particular thematic questions. You are asked "what matters to you?"

The chapter then turns to ask "what matters to us?" You are presented with ways the UCC has lived and expressed each vital theme—and then there are more questions. How does "what matters to you" link with and challenge "what matters to us" and vice versa. How does "what matters to us" affirm and engage "what matters to you"? We want to engage fully in a conversation with you— both of us growing because of the questions and faith that are shared.

WHAT MATTERS TO US?
Six Vital Themes

- We are people of God's extravagant welcome.

- We belong to Christ.

- We are a people of covenant, a united and uniting church.

- We are one at Baptism and the Table.

- We thank God by working for a just and loving world.

- We listen for the still-speaking God.

Chapters also include ways to pray, to study the Bible, and to act for God's justice. Inquiring in faith isn't just for the head, but for the heart and will as well. Try out the ways of praying. Explore ways to express God's justice. Go deeper.

The chapter "Our History Matters" offers brief stories from our past that exemplify the six vital themes. Rather than a chronological history of the UCC, you will discover moments in our history when we "lived the questions." We were presented with a choice and responded— sometimes, by God's grace, full of faith, and sometimes full of fear. Read the chapter completely or as you read each theme chapter, take time to read the stories from "Our History Matters" that express the particular theme.

At the conclusion of each chapter, you'll see several notes that point to sources as well as relevant online addresses. For further exploration of the themes and historical accounts, link to these important sites.

If at all possible, join with others in asking questions and exploring faith. Whom might God call you to join for conversation and friendship? If you are not part of a UCC congregation, consider discovering one online at "Find a Church" at www.ucc.org/find/. Or participate in an online UCC community at i.ucc.org/Home/tabid/36/Default.aspx. Become a part of a community of inquiry, of deepening faith. The UCC affirms communities of covenant—believing God's word can be heard in powerful, comforting, and challenging ways when we bind ourselves together to listen to God and one another. Suggestions for using this resource in groups or congregations are found at www.united churchpress.com.

What Matters to You? Matters to Us was developed through the questions, prayers, interviews, and discernment with others as well. We have asked, "What resources might help those who are seekers, those desiring to deepen their faith, or those who wonder about the UCC?" The online article at www.unitedchurchpress.com describes the questions and concerns of inquirers, visitors, and seekers. We wondered about those who were discovering the UCC for the first time as a result of the "God Is Still Speaking" campaign and ads. Out of conversations around the church—loving the questions that emerged—a brochure was developed that first highlighted the six vital UCC themes of who we are.[2]

We continued to ask questions. We discovered how vital UCC congregations and members express those themes. We explored our history for stories of those themes. We identified how biblical grounding, prayers, worship possibilities, and acts of justice link with the themes. The online study guide *What Matters* (available online at www.uccvitality.org) was created. This book grows out of that work.

It's true. No matter where you are on your journey of faith, you are welcome in the United Church of Christ. *You* matter. Together, let's live the questions. The grace of God is yours.

NOTES

1. Rainer Maria Rilke, *Letters to a Young Poet,* translated by Stephen Mitchell (New York: Vintage Books, 1984) 34–35.

2. To order *What Matters to You?* brochures, call toll free, 800-537-3394. Cost: $15.00 per bundle of fifty. Order #LCMCV1 for brochures with assorted covers, #LCMCV1E for "What Matters to You? Matters to Us" cover, #LCMCV1A for "Find Yourself. We Have GPS" cover, #LCMV1B for "Our Faith is 2000 Years Old, Our Thinking Is Not" cover, #LCMCV1C "Please Return" cover, or #LCMCV1D for "United Not Divided" cover. For a set of six posters—one for each theme, order #LCMCVIO, $6.00.

Come, share your journey with us.

No matter who you are or where you are on life's journey, you're welcome here.

1 we are people of God's extravagant welcome

WHAT MATTERS TO YOU?

When you enter a room, usually you realize fairly quickly whether you are welcome or not. Something about the people or the environment—what is said or done, not said or not done—lets you know. Will you high-tail it out of the place, silently endure the meeting for the time being, or settle in feeling a bit at home? When the welcome is warm, sincere, generous—extravagant—you just may have discovered a people and place that you want to know more deeply. Lately we stated in a United Church of Christ ad that "No matter who you are or where you are on life's journey, you're welcome here." As a door to discovering whether that statement is true or not for you, take some time to consider your own experiences of being welcomed.

- When was a time that you felt especially welcomed? What did people do to make you feel welcome?

- Have you known a time when it was tough to be hospitable to another? When?

- When did your church especially demonstrate an extravagant welcome?

- When and where have you experienced God as welcoming?

WHAT MATTERS TO US

"Jesus didn't turn people away, neither do we." When you're gutsy enough to make such a claim, it's not always easy to make good on it. Following Jesus' lead, the United Church of Christ strives to keep doors open to all. By God's grace—in the past and today—we do what needs to be done to be bold people of God's welcome.

Jesus, indeed, lived and breathed gracious hospitality. Even though there were powerful people who opposed Jesus' extravagant welcome, he still embraced those who were often shunned. In the reign of God that Jesus spoke of, he declared there is room for all—children (Luke 18:15–17) and those who are hungry, thirsty, homeless, ill, poor, grieving, persecuted, and in prison (Matthew 25:31–46 and Luke 6:20–26). Jesus put faith and hospitality together: "Whoever receives one whom I send receives me," and those who received Jesus, embraced God (John 13:20).

This kind of hospitality is characteristic of both God's faithfulness and, at our best, our faithfulness. God welcomes and also feeds the hungry, forgives sins, stands with those who are poor and oppressed, comforts those suffering, and becomes home for those who wander. In gratitude, faithful people welcome strangers. Actually, in the Bible, the way you welcome a stranger expresses how you embrace the very presence of God (Genesis 18:1–8 and Luke 23:28–35).

The church, since its beginning, continues to "extend hospitality to strangers" (Romans 12:13). The church, after all, is a blessed company of strangers held together by the grace of God. UCC churches express God's extravagant welcome in a variety of ways. Our welcome embraces those we invite to participate in our congregations, as well as those outside the church, with whom we work for God's justice and compassion. Such hospitality is our prayer, our hope.

Who is welcome? Our churches are among those whose doors are open to God's children of different cultures, races, genders, ages, sexual orientations, abilities, economic situations, and theological traditions. It isn't always easy to be so open. Each UCC congregation prayerfully discerns and expresses how wide their doors and arms are open.

Some state it this way, "We are multicultural and multiracial, open and affirming, accessible to all, and a peace with justice church." That's a mouthful, yet the phrase sums up our commitments through the years. We are multicultural and multiracial including a beautiful mosaic of witnesses from various racial, ethnic, cultural, and national communities. We are open and affirming, having been on the forefront of embracing the ministry of lesbian, gay, bisexual, and transgender people of faith. We are accessible to all, taking seriously the gifts of those with various physical and mental abilities and assuring that full participation is possible. We are a peace with justice church. Not only do we attempt to be welcoming in our congregations, we seek to make the world more welcoming to all God's children by working for justice and peace. Each of these commitments is visible in the work of the national setting of the UCC, but also in many local congregations.[1] What about yours?

Once one enters the door, it's not a matter of "sit back, be quiet, and speak only as we do." You, your heart's questions, and your gifts are vital to the congregation. We both grow together in faith and witness. Your distinct story of faith joins with centuries of stories that make up the church, and specifically the United Church of Christ. In God's grace, you change; we change. We make a holy difference in each other's lives and, together, in the world.

In gratitude because God welcomes us, we are called to make bold stands. On behalf of and along with those who remain oppressed, suffering, alienated, and poor in God's world, we speak and act. "It's not an extravagant welcome to an 'anything-goes' religion, a comfortable form of Christianity, but to a costly form of discipleship," says John Thomas, president and general minister of the UCC. Thomas calls this kind of discipleship "evangelical courage." It's the other side of the "extravagant welcome" coin. You see this risky faith expressed throughout our history that at times has been hidden. Discover such stories from our past in chapter 7, "Our History Matters," page 51. Inspired by God's gift of hospitality, we work for God's welcoming world of love and justice.

- What do you find encouraging about the United Church of Christ and our commitment to God's extravagant welcome?

- Who do you pray might walk through your church's door? If they entered, what difference might it make to your church, to you, to them?

- What is God calling you and your church to do or say to create a more welcoming and just world?

PRAYER MATTERS

Intercessory Prayer ▪ *A Welcoming Prayer*

Prayer, itself, is a form of "extravagant welcome." Most often when we pray, it is family, friends, and those we know who come to mind. However, prayer of the extravagant welcome or true intercessory prayer opens us to all God's children and the world around us.

Spend time in prayer by first opening yourself to God, then asking God to draw to heart and mind those for whom God would have you pray. Whose faces and what situations come to mind? Who in our world longs for your prayers? Be open to the rich diversity of people whom God embraces and their life situations.

Tell God your hopes for these people and situations. But also be silent, and simply be aware of them in the presence of God. With these persons in your heart, what might God be calling from you? God may move us from hearts open in prayer to actions of extravagant welcome.

BIBLE MATTERS

Matthew 25:34–45 ▪ *The Least of These*

Begin in prayer, asking God to be present with you as you explore Matthew 25:34–45.

Read the passage aloud. Follow with a moment of silence.

Read the passage again, pausing from time to time when a word or image seems to stick in your mind or heart. Offer the thought to God or briefly pray about the image or word.

Consider that in Matthew's prophetic vision Jesus completely identifies with those who are hungry, thirsty, strangers, naked, or in prison. All are surprised when they are either praised or judged on how they welcomed Jesus in "the least of these."

Prayerfully reflect: What good news is in the passages? What is disturbing? What might God be saying to me and our church about God's extravagant welcome?

PEOPLE MATTER

"The world is desperate for a word of welcome and grace . . . so we are a people of extravagant welcome." —*John H. Thomas, general minister and president of the United Church of Christ, Cleveland, Ohio*

"Every Sunday, Molly glides into a church where she is loved and accepted. I know there is a community there to support her and that makes me want to support it back even more. It is our mission to be a blessing to others as God has been to us. Through the church, my family feels accepted, nurtured and cared for—we feel whole." —*Bernie, father of Molly who has cerebral palsy and is wheelchair-bound*

"By never backing down on our church's commitment to welcome, it's tough at times. It's impossible to come away without being challenged in some way. Church isn't business as usual. It's worth it, however. The United Church of Christ is a godsend." —*Kathy McCallie, pastor, Church of the Open Arms UCC, Oklahoma City, Oklahoma*

GOD'S WORLD MATTERS

Welcoming the World

Extravagant welcome is not only a matter of opening doors of your congregation. It is a commitment to make the world a more hospitable place for God's children. Explore both the current global plight of refugees and that of immigrants into the United States. In your own community, how are immigrants received? How might God be calling you and your congregation to respond? The United Church of Christ is involved in various actions.[2]

NOTES

1. *Shine God's People* is a five-unit study of these historic UCC commitments, available from UCCR, toll free at 800.537.3394 (order #LCMCV2) or online at www.ucc.org/50/resources/study-guide.html. For additional online information about the commitment to be a multiracial and multicultural church, visit www.ucc.org/justice/racism/multiracial-multicultural.html; to be an open and affirming congregation, see www.ucc.org/lgbt/ or www.ucc.org/lgbt/ona.html; to be a church accessible to all, see www.uccdm.org/; and to be a peace with justice church, see www.ucc.org/justice/join-the-network/ and www.globalministries.org or www.ucc.org/justice/peacemaking/a-just-peace-church-1.html.

2. For more information, link to www.ucc.org/refugees/ or contact the executive for refugee ministries, Wider Church Ministries (216.736.3212). At its 2007 Twenty-sixth General Synod, the UCC adopted a resolution on immigration reform (link to www.ucc.org/synod/resolutions/immigration-final.pdf.).

How do you know God? Tell us your story.
Let's grow together.

Grounded in our history and open to the future
with you, our heart belongs to Christ.

2 we belong to Christ

WHAT MATTERS TO YOU

You have a choice. You decide. With questions, doubts, hopes, and prayers, each of us decides whether or not to answer the question, "Are you Christian?" with a "Yes" or with a "No." Each of us then explains the "yes" and the "no" with words and actions that seem to make sense of, or at least reflects, the truth and love we know. The United Church of Christ believes you're not alone in the seeking and deciding. God, who gave you breath, abides with you in your searching. The UCC also joins you in looking to Jesus Christ—for grace, courage, prayer, for asking the tough questions, for a life of both joy and discipleship.

- What questions do you have about Jesus Christ?
- At different points in your life what did you think or wonder about Jesus? What about God?
- Describe a time when you experienced God or Christ in your life.
- When someone says, "I'm Christian," what does it usually mean to you?
- If you say, "I'm a Christian," what do you mean?

WHAT MATTERS TO US

"We belong to Christ" is a loaded phrase. It's loaded because it means different things to different people. It packs within it comfort for some, challenge for others. For many, it includes the constant and curious combination of both comfort and challenge. For some, the words unite; for others the words divide. In the United Church of Christ, we pray the words comfort, challenge, and unite.

Simply put, the "we" in the phrase means you are not alone. You are part of the larger "we" that God has united into the United Church of Christ. "Belongs" is something more than belief; it's a vital relationship. It's not like belonging to a club where hazing or proven credentials or social standing are required. It's more like belonging to a nurturing parent, family, or community. Belonging is a relational gift that inspires thanks and devotion.

And what about the words "to Christ"? God, to whom we belong, is understood and experienced by Christians through Jesus Christ. In the Bible, we discover the story and witness of Christ. God is known in Jesus, infant and child; in the Galilean man's ministry and teaching; and in Christ's death and resurrection. Jesus Christ is prophet (Luke 4:14–30), teacher (Matthew 5), healer (Mark 5:21–43), savior (John 3:16), welcoming host (Mark 8:1–11), justice-doer (Luke 19:1–27), a pray-er (Luke 22:39–44), a dying servant (John 19:28–30), and a living companion along the way (Luke 24:13–35). In the gospel of John, Jesus is our bread, living water, door, and light. Christ is the way, truth, and life. We discover much about Jesus in scripture, but we also experience Jesus today.

For us in the UCC, this relationship to Jesus Christ embraces us as individuals, as a church, and as we relate to the world. An early teaching found in the Heidelberg Catechism, part of our German Reformed heritage, asked individuals: "What is your only comfort in life and death?" The response was "That I belong—body and soul, in life and death—not to myself, but to my faithful Savior, Jesus Christ. . . ." (Discover more about the catechism in chapter 7, "Our History Matters," page 55.) Joined to Christ, we enjoy life abundant and hope even beyond death. Today, we too are formed in Christ.

Our name, United Church of Christ, was chosen not because we intended to exclude people, but rather to embrace the world as widely as Jesus' own arms embrace the world.[1] No one person, creed, statement, denomination, or church holds all truth—only Christ, only God. What we say about God in Christ "begins in wonder, and when theological thought has done its best, the wonder remains."[2]

God is not an object to be contained, but a holy mystery to encounter together. In praying honestly and listening openly, in tasting bread together at Holy Communion, in hearing good news proclaimed, and at the flowing waters of baptism, we meet Jesus. Where there is justice, peace, and compassion, we see the living God at work. To such a God, we belong; you belong.

Although Christ is the primary lens through which we view God, we experience God in a variety of ways. Through the centuries and with many other churches, one way that we have talked about God is through the Trinity of Father, Son, and Holy Spirit. You hear this in ancient creeds, as the Apostles' and Nicene creeds,[3] as well as in our contemporary UCC "Statement of Faith." (Read the entire "Statement of Faith" on pages 76–77.)

The Trinity expresses many ways God relates to us, and we relate to God. Yes, we believe in one God, but our God is dynamic, inviting, intimate, and communal, not stuck in only one aspect. God exhibits diversity. The Holy One is known in the diverse expressions of God's parental and creative care, Christ's eternal justice and compassion, and the Spirit's power and abiding presence.

We also speak about God in other ways that enrich our faith— God as mother, rock, liberator, savior, and friend. These understandings, affirmed in the Bible, break through any single, limited way of experiencing God and open us to be changed in new ways by this marvelous God.

Grounded in our history and open to the future with you, our heart belongs to Christ. Turn to chapter 7, "Our History Matters" (page 55), to discover how we have come to understand Christ throughout our history. We affirm historic creeds and statements of faith, not as demanding tests, but as inspired words of faithful women and men who came before us. We continue to discover God through the Bible, through prayer, through worship, through engaging in the world in just and loving ways. We especially listen for the voice of God in the voices of those who cry out for justice and peace. We intend to follow Christ faithfully into the world.

- How do you imagine Christ?

- Who is the Christ to whom you belong?

- What might God be saying to you as you consider "We belong to Christ"?

- How do you figure your congregation understands that they "belong to Christ"? Why?

- What do you want to learn more about?

PRAYER MATTERS

The Prayer of Our Savior ▪ *Belonging to Jesus*

What we pray are not empty words. The words we use in prayer—no matter how simple or complex—express much of what we believe, what we are grateful for, as well as deep longings. In the gospel of Luke, Jesus' followers ask of him: "Teach us to pray" (11:1-4). Jesus responds with a prayer that holds within it his longings, beliefs, and hopes about God and the entire world. When we pray the prayer, when we utter the words, when we pray as Jesus prayed, we draw close to him.

Slow down your praying of the Prayer of Our Savior. Begin with deep breaths, aware of the gift of life from God. Aware that you draw close to Jesus and his vision of God's realm when you pray, slowly offer the words. Pause often after a word or phrase to hold it in your heart, express your thoughts and feelings to God, and open yourself to God speaking to you. At times, consider praying the prayer over a day or week—holding only one word or phrase as the single focus in a time of prayer. This prayerful practice may also enrich your praying when you pray the Prayer of Our Savior with your congregation.

Use the following ecumenical version of the prayer or a familiar version used when your congregation prays together. You may also wish to begin your prayer with the additional words in italic.

Held in the arms of God, our Mother, I pray the prayer of Jesus, brother,
savior, and friend:

Our Father in heaven,
hallowed be your name,
your kingdom come, your will be done,
on earth as in heaven.
Give us today our daily bread.
Forgive us our sins as we forgive those who sin against us.
Save us from the time of trial,
and deliver us from evil.
For the kingdom, the power, and the glory are yours
now and for ever.
Amen.[4]

BIBLE MATTERS

Romans 14:7–8 ▪ *Whether We Live or Die, We Belong to Christ*

Begin exploring Romans 14:7–8 with a time of silent prayer and deep breathing. Become aware of your breath. Slowly with each breath, offer thanks to God for the gift of life.

Read Romans 14:7–8 slowly aloud. Pause after your first reading and then read again.

Reflect on "O God, what questions, challenge, or comfort do these words conjure up in me?"

Consider: In the fourteenth chapter of the book of Romans, the author Paul dealt directly with conflict within the church at Rome. One group of Christians followed certain dietary practices; others did not. Paul called on the community to welcome one another, not to judge or despise one another, and to pursue peace in building up one another. Verses 7–8 are the basis for openness to one another. Belonging to Christ draws individuals into a community where each is regarded as vital to the body of Christ. Those in the Roman church were reminded that their lives in Christ were not about only their own interests, but Christ's. The reminder was both a comfort—that even beyond death they share in Christ's resurrection—and a challenge—that life is not about satisfying their own desires, but Christ's.

Once again, reflect on the challenge and comfort of the passage. What might God be saying to you or your congregation? Finally, rest in God—perhaps with a hand on your chest and silently repeating the words "I belong to Christ."

PEOPLE MATTER

"I can now say that I am a true believer in my own right—that I belong to Christ. I know I can call on Christ in difficult times and give all my struggles to him—no matter the situation. —*Robin Sadler, young adult member of Mount Zion, Cleveland, Ohio*

"We have many christologies, many beliefs, many interpretations of the Bible, but we are one in Christ. What one believes should not be held as a test for another, but as a testimony of one's own faith." —*Lourdino Yuzon, pastor of Carrollton Cosmopolitan UCC in Carrollton, Texas, describing how his congregation moved through conflict*

"I remember the chorus, 'Now I belong to Jesus, Jesus belongs to me . . .' We in the UCC are to be driven by the words, the spirit, and the example of Jesus Christ." —*José A. Malayang, former executive minister, Local Church Ministries, UCC, Cleveland, Ohio*

GOD'S WORLD MATTERS

Racial Justice as Belonging to Christ

Belonging to Christ means that we are also bound to others who belong to Christ. Together, sisters and brothers all, we are created in the image of God. Throughout our history, we have linked belonging to Christ to advocating for racial justice and eradicating racism. At the 2003 General Synod, we affirmed this heritage when we officially adopted the call to be an antiracist church.[5] This action called for work from the national setting of our church, but also from local congregations. Churches were called on to develop programs that examine both historic and contemporary forms of racism and its effects.

Since 1991, we have also worked against racial stereotyping and the immense damage it does to individuals and society. For example, the use of Native Americans as logos and mascots especially in sports and corporate settings. We state, "As Christians, we must challenge the use of Native Americans as caricatures, and instead honor all human beings as created in the image and likeness of God."[6] Belonging to Christ and bound to one another, how do you and your congregation witness to these vital relationships through working for racial justice?

NOTES

1. "Basis of Union," *The Living Theological Heritage*, vol. 6, ed. Elisabeth Slaughter Hilke (Cleveland: Pilgrim Press, 2001), Doc. 77, 583–84.

2. Allen O. Miller, "The Mystery of God and Humanity," *The Living Theological Heritage*, vol. 7, eds. Frederick R. Trost and Barbara Brown Zikmund (Cleveland: Pilgrim Press), Doc. 80, 430.

3. For the Apostles and Nicene Creeds, visit online www.ucc.org/beliefs/the-apostles-creed.html and www.ucc.org/beliefs/nicene-creed.html.

4. International Consultation on English Texts, also found in *Book of Worship: United Church of Christ*, reprint, (Cleveland: Local Church Ministries, Local Church Ministries, 2002), 516.

5. "Adopted 2003 General Synod Multiracial/Multicultural Addendum to 1993 Pronouncement and Proposal for Action," online at www.ucc.org/justice/racism/anti-racist-church.html.

6. For more information about UCC involvement in combating negative racial stereotyping, visit http://www.ucc.org/justice/racism/negative-stereotyping.html.

All are welcome into a special relationship with God, especially you.

The Holy Spirit binds in covenant faithful people of all ages, tongues, and races.

3 we are a people of covenant, a united and uniting church

WHAT MATTERS TO YOU?

What relationships bring you great joy? When it comes to friendship, partnership, marriage, community, and church, you know it's good when it's nurtured in love, honesty, and trust. The United Church of Christ believes that distinctive quality of relationship isn't just for those most intimate to you—it is also how we relate to one another, to other churches, to the world. Such quality relationships mirror the relationship God desires to have with us.

- What relationships matter to you that involve a promise?
- How is God involved in the relationship?
- How do promises, covenants, help hold things together in tough times?

WHAT MATTERS TO US

What is it that holds people together even in the midst of all kinds of differences? When folks in the UCC talk about how they relate — to God, each other, other churches, other religions, even creation—they often use the word "covenant." It's God's good glue that keeps us together. Covenant is a holy promise of devotion that is shared. When that glue sticks, God forms a bond of unity that is pliable and dynamic, not rigid or unresponsive. Unity is a result of a covenantal way of life and an amazing gift of God.

In the Bible, God covenants. At the end of the story of Noah and the flood, God covenants and a rainbow appears (Genesis 9:8–17). When God liberates the Hebrews from slavery in Egypt, God covenants, Moses delivers the commandments, and Miriam celebrates the covenant with dance (Exodus 15 and Deuteronomy 6:11–25, 7:7–11). Covenant isn't any legal document written in stone, but is to be taken to heart (Jeremiah 31:31). Covenant includes devoted actions promised between God and people. Covenant is also lived between the people of God through friendship, love, and loyalty. Such a relational covenant is seen between the biblical hero David and the ruler's son, Jonathan (1 Samuel 18:3), and between the widow Ruth and her mother-in-law, Naomi (Ruth 1:16–18).

The covenant continues in Jesus. Jesus Christ is the new covenant expressed at Holy Communion when Jesus' presence is poured out on God's people (Matthew 26:28, 1 Corinthians 11:23). Our participation in the new covenant leads us to join as partners in Christ's reconciliation in the world.

Like covenant, unity is a significant theme in the Bible and to the UCC. It is so central to us that Jesus' prayer in John 17, "that they may be one," is the prayer inscribed on our logo. In our "Statement of Faith" (page 76), covenant is a gift of the Holy Spirit "binding in covenant faithful people of all ages, tongues, and races." We celebrate this every time there is a baptism or we gather for Holy Communion. The first word when we utter our name, "United Church of Christ," expresses our yearning for covenant: "United!"

Covenant is how we relate to one another within local churches, and it is much more than that. Both covenant and unity have been in our UCC heart since we formed in 1957, and they run through our blood because of our historical foreparents. Discover how they lived out their covenants early in our history by turning to chapter 7, "Our History Matters" (page 57).

In the 2001 edition of our Constitution, covenant is the foundation for our way of being the church. Each congregation has "autonomy," meaning it's free to discern its own way of being and believing. Yet, because of covenant, we bind ourselves to one another beyond the local church—to associations, conferences, the national setting, and General Synod. And, guess what? Those settings are called to covenant with your congregation. The constitution puts it this way: "Each expression of the church listens, hears, and carefully considers the advice, counsel, and requests of others. In this covenant, the various expressions of the United Church of Christ walk together in all God's ways."[1]

Another word similar to "unity" that expresses covenant is "ecumenical." Usually it points toward unity, or the desire for unity, among all Christian churches throughout the world. We are not only a united church, we are a uniting church. This doesn't mean all churches become alike, or one is swallowed up by another. Instead churches come together, each with its own distinct gifts, to more fully express Christ in the world.

For us in the UCC, "ecumenicity is not an option."[2] It is essential. We demonstrate it in a network of partnerships and councils with other churches. A few of those relationships include the World Council of Churches, the National Council of Churches, the Ecumenical Partnership with the Christian Church (Disciples of Christ), the Formula of Agreement (Lutheran/Reformed), and Churches Uniting in Christ.

Do we also enter into a covenantal way with other world religions? More than ever, we encounter persons deeply devoted to their own faiths—other than Christian. In the past, missionary efforts were primary in approaching other faiths. Our efforts included assisting with health care, education, and working for justice, but often we did not tolerate God's gifts through other religions or cultures. Today, we seek prayerful discernment and conversation together—open to God seeking us in new ways.

Because we are people of covenant, we also value diversity and the variety of gifts. We are bound to all God's children. Beyond relationships, our covenant way of life extends to how we care for the earth, which cradles our very existence. Mack Stokes has described covenant as a "gift of God that bonds the human will to God's justice and to the neighbor. . . ."[3] Our prayer for unity extends beyond the unity of all churches to the reconciliation of God's whole world.

Our covenant way of life is personal and public, pastoral and political, local and global. At times all this covenanting and uniting isn't so easy to figure out. A commitment to one group conflicts with the covenant with another. We become torn in a way so that the glue grows brittle and the bond is ready to break. Then with humility, we struggle with God and neighbor about what is faithful. When it holds, we declare, "Thanks be to God!" Covenant is a way of living.

- Where is brokenness in our world that yearns for reconciliation?
- With whom or what is God calling us to covenant?

PRAYER MATTERS

A Rule of Life ▪ *Living a Daily Covenant*

Living a covenant way of life calls for prayer and discipline. One practice that may help you tend to your covenants is the ancient practice called "A Rule of Life." One of the most famous rules was "The Rule of St. Benedict," but you can prayerfully identify your own. A rule usually includes a list of what matters—things to do as well as things to keep in your mind and heart—which assists in deepening your life of covenant. Although you might mistake the rule for some kind of "New Year's resolutions," instead what you identify comes out of prayer and what God calls you to nurture. What do you feel led to include? Your rule might include: to pray daily (even if not certain of the number of times or length of time available) and to prayerfully examine, at least once a week, how you live your covenants with God and others. Martin Luther King Jr. developed his own Rule of Life that included such practices as these: "Walk and talk in the manner of love, for God is love," "Seek to perform regular service to others and the world," and "Refrain from violence of fist, tongue, or heart."[4]

BIBLE MATTERS

John 17:21b–23 ▪ *That They May All Be One*

Begin your study of Jesus' prayer in John 17 with silent prayer. Open yourself to God speaking to you. Take a moment to imagine Jesus at prayer. The "hour has come" (John 17:1b) and Jesus now faces the end of his life. He lifts up his heart to God and prays for those who come after him, his apostles and the church.

Read John 17:21b–23 and hear the words as if spoken by Jesus. Pause and read again.

In silence, consider what Jesus' words conjure up in you. What is your prayer after hearing Jesus' prayer?

Consider: These verses are from Jesus' much longer prayer that fills the entire seventeenth chapter of John. The chapter blends proclamation as well as prayer. Here we listen to Jesus' prayer before his death, but also to the risen Christ's call to the church. Jesus links who he is with who God is. They are one. That unity is continued into the future through Jesus' followers, but also through the church. The continuity of God's way of love is discovered in uniting Christ and us, the entire church, as we unite in living God's love and justice in the world.

Once again, move into silence. Discern "After exploring Christ's prayer for unity, what is your own prayer? What is your prayer for the church?"

Conclude your time by saying aloud the following prayer affirmation or one in your own words: "Holy One, we pray that all may be one. Amen."

PEOPLE MATTER

"They joined together, not because they had to or because of financial considerations, but because they felt God called them to unite." *—Don Childers, pastor of the United Church of Los Alamos, Los Alamos, New Mexico, describing his congregation, which includes formal relationship with six denominations, including the UCC*

"Here our covenantal relationship is affirmed and blessed and we feel woven into the very fabric of the open and affirming spirit of the UCC." *—Mary Etta Perry, describing*

First Congregational UCC, Asheville, North Carolina, where she and Mary Cowal, her partner for more than thirty-five years, are members.

"Together we reconcile ourselves and others to the wholeness and abundance of God's peace joining the four corners of the world—in recognition of God's love and common concern for all." —*Linda Jaramillo, executive minister for Justice and Witness Ministries, United Church of Christ, Cleveland, Ohio*

GOD'S WORLD MATTERS

United for Peace ▪ *Church World Service in Darfur*

God calls us into partnerships that unite denominations, congregations, and communities across the globe. One such place is the Darfur region of Sudan, an area torn by civil strife that has led to the deaths of hundreds of thousands of people and left thousands more displaced from their homes. The desperate situation in the Darfur has led to interfaith partnerships that span the political spectrum in an effort to provide humanitarian aid for the refugees and advance the cause of peace.

A primary way that the UCC joins with others is through Church World Service (CWS) efforts. This relief organization joins more than thirty-five Protestant, Orthodox, and Anglican denominations in partnership with indigenous organizations in more than eighty countries. Discover how you and your congregation may unite in an effort to bring healing to the Darfur. For specific information, visit online http://www.ucc.org/disaster/ and www.churchworldservice.org.

NOTES

1. The *Constitution and Bylaws: United Church of Christ,* 2000 edition (Cleveland: Executive Council for the United Church of Christ, 2000), 3. Also visit online http://www.ucc.org/about-us/constitution-of-the-ucc.html#COVENANT.

2. "Ecumenical Stance of the United Church of Christ," *The Living Theological Library,* vol. 7, eds. Frederick R. Trost and Barbara Brown Zikmund (Cleveland: Pilgrim Press, 2005), Doc. 103, 571.

3. Max L. Stackhouse, "Covenantal Relationships," *The Living Theological Library,* vol. 7, eds. Frederick R. Trost and Barbara Brown Zikmund (Cleveland: Pilgrim Press, 2005), Doc. 140, 773.

4. Identified in Marjorie J. Thompson, *Soul Feast: An Invitation to the Christian Spiritual Life* (Louisville: Westminster John Knox Press, 1995), 140.

Come to the water of baptism and the table of Christ. Receive God's goodness and love.

The Holy Spirit through water, bread, and wine makes visible the grace, forgiveness, and presence of God in Christ.

4 we are one at baptism and the table

WHAT MATTERS TO YOU

The first time you visit worship in a church, you usually wonder what's going to happen next and what it means. Even if something happens that feels a bit familiar, you never fully seem to grasp it. For example, you've washed with water. You've eaten bread. What can and do these ordinary daily activities mean when they occur in worship? What is God about—even with you?

- What are all the ways we use and experience water, bread, and wine?

- How might those experiences also describe an experience of God?

- What is your experience of God and those in your congregation while participating in baptism or Holy Communion?

WHAT MATTERS TO US

Just some water, just a simple meal of bread and juice, but for us in the United Church of Christ, what is simple means much more. These basic elements of life take on profound significance when blessed by the Holy Spirit and celebrated within Christ's church. Flowing water becomes the sacrament of baptism. A meal of bread and wine becomes the sacrament of Holy Communion. In these two sacraments, we see, touch, and taste the love, forgiveness, covenant, and presence of God in Christ.[1]

The preamble of our Constitution states that the UCC "recognizes" these two sacraments (see page 75). Recognition, however, is more than a mere casual acknowledgement. Recognition is a deep way of seeing and experiencing God and God's action. Recognition recalls Jesus Christ and his own baptism (Mark 1:9–11), his call to baptize others (Matthew 28:16–20), and the invitation to become one with Christ and one another in baptism (Romans 6:1–4). Recognition remembers Jesus' meals with his followers and his Last Supper (Luke 22:7–13), discovers his continuing presence in the breaking of bread (Luke 24:30–31a), and anticipates a great banquet for all God's people (Luke 14:15–24). Recognition is not only an individual act, but one we share with Christians throughout the world.

What happens at baptism and Holy Communion? What do they mean? Our *Book of Worship* and the words we use to celebrate the sacraments reflect a variety of meanings. These understandings we share in common with many other Christians, and they are also reflected in the World Council of Churches' ecumenical agreement called *Baptism, Eucharist and Ministry.*[2]

Through water at baptism, God embraces you—no matter who you are—and brings you into Christ's church. You become vital to not only a local church, but also the wider church. You share in the life, death, and resurrection of Christ. The church also promises to love, support, and care for you throughout your whole life. Baptized, you now participate fully in the life of the church and God's realm.

At Holy Communion, we do share a simple meal of bread and wine. Yet in the meal, we experience the presence of Christ again. Together, around God's welcome table, we recall God's loving acts especially in Jesus, experience our oneness in Christ, hope for a time when all will be fed, and anticipate the fullness of God's love and justice throughout creation.

How we "do" the sacraments varies among our congregations. A 2004–2006 UCC worship survey detailed that range of practices.[3] Some congregations baptize people of all ages—from infants through adults. Others begin baptism with older children. All use water, but the amount varies from a small amount to full immersion in a body of water. Often a pastor baptizes with the ecumenical wording "in the name of the Father, Son, and Holy Spirit." Others use additional expressions—including feminine imagery—of the Triune God. Almost in all cases, baptism occurs within a worshiping congregation and, as initiation into the church, occurs only once.

The number of times a church celebrates Holy Communion ranges from seldom to weekly, but it is usually celebrated monthly. Some use a common loaf of bread and a cup; others use wafers and small communion cups. Some receive communion in the pews, others join together at the front of the worship space. Some congregations reserve communion for those who are both baptized and confirmed, while others invite all regardless of baptism or confirmation. Increasingly children are welcome to communion at their parent's discretion.

All the themes of our faith seem to come together in the sacraments. Christ claims us, and we belong to Christ. God offers an extravagant welcome, and we share in it. God keeps covenant with us, and we unite as one with Christians throughout the world. God offers a vision of justice and love, and we are inspired to live it. Notice the rich history of the sacraments in the chapter "Our History Matters" page 60. Together, through water, bread, and wine, we know the still-speaking God.

- From your own experience of baptism and Holy Communion, what do they mean to you? How might the meanings have changed over time?

- When have you participated in a baptism or Holy Communion that was particularly meaningful? Pray a prayer such as "O God, what are you saying and revealing to us about our own congregation's practice of the sacraments?"

PRAYER MATTERS

Blessing of Water ▪ *Praying and Living Your Baptism*

In the UCC, we have a prayer found in our *Book of Worship* that is often used in blessing water at baptism. It is a beautiful retelling of God's blessing of water throughout history. When we are baptized, we participate again in all of God's water stories of deliverance. The following prayer practice is not intended to "imitate" baptism, but to assist in preparing for baptism. The prayer also invites you to recall your baptism anytime that you taste, touch, or see water.

Breathe deeply, aware of God's presence, and pour water in a small basin.

Pray the words of the prayer slowly, pausing often during the verses. Imagine the stories of salvation "rising" from the water.

At the end of the words, dip your hands in the water and fold them in prayer. Continue to pray in silence, open to God, sensitive to any understandings, feelings, or convictions that may emerge.

Thanksgiving and Blessing over the Water[4]

We thank you, God, for the gift of creation called forth by your
    saving Word.
Before the world had shape and form, your Spirit moved over
    the waters.
Out of the waters of the deep, you formed the firmament and brought forth earth
    to sustain life.
In the time of Noah,
you washed the earth with the waters of the flood,
and your ark of salvation bore a new beginning.
In the time of Moses [, Aaron, and Miriam],
our people Israel passed through the Red Sea waters
from slavery to freedom and crossed the flowing Jordan
to enter the promised land.
In the fullness of time, you sent Jesus Christ,
who was nurtured in the water of Mary's womb.
Jesus was baptized by John in the water of the Jordan,
became living water to a woman at the Samaritan well,
washed the feet of the disciples,
and sent them forth to baptize all nations by water and the Holy Spirit.
Bless by your Holy Spirit, gracious God, this water.
By your Holy Spirit save those who confess the name of Jesus Christ

that sin may have no power over them.
Create new life in the one/all baptized this day
that she/he/they may rise in Christ.
Glory to you, eternal God,
the one who was, and is, and shall always be,
world without end. Amen.

BIBLE MATTERS

1 Corinthians 11:17–33 ▪ *Community in Communion*

Begin with a time of silence. Ask God to guide your understanding of scripture.

Slowly read 1 Corinthians 11:17–33 aloud.

Ask yourself: What comforts or disturbs me about this passage? What seems to be at stake here? If I were to paint a picture of Holy Communion among the folk at Corinth, what do I guess it would look like?

Consider the setting of Paul's writing to the church at Corinth. The church was more divided than united as they participated in Holy Communion. The sacramental meal was part of a common meal where some gorged on food and drink, and others went hungry. Rather than a time that expressed oneness in Christ, it highlighted a division between those who had much and those who had little. Paul connects Holy Communion with the ethical implications of the sacrament by pointing back to Jesus' sharing at the Last Supper. That supper expressed Christ's life offered on behalf of others. True participation in Christ's meal invited such an offering of self—transforming unjust relationships as well as personal "hungers." Paul called on the Corinthians to partake in the meal in a worthy manner: "Examine yourselves, and only then eat of the bread and drink of the cup" (verse 28).

Prayerfully reflect on questions such as these: How is your congregation different from or similar to the Corinthians'? How do you prepare to participate in Holy Communion? What might it mean for you and your congregation to examine yourselves? What are the differences that Holy Communion might make both to individuals and to the church?

Enter silence again. Be aware of any thoughts or insights that occur during prayer.

| **PEOPLE MATTER**

"In baptism and Holy Communion we become a part of something intimate and something larger than we are." — *John H. Thomas, general minister and president, United Church of Christ, Cleveland, Ohio*

"At communion, when that private moment comes when we receive the bread and juice, we are squeezed right next to somebody else. Older members are squeezed right next to children and youth. Folks not only nod at each other at the rail, but when tears begin to fall from someone's face, there is another to embrace them and help them with a tissue or two." — *James Fouther, pastor, United Church of Montbello, Denver, Colorado*

"I always involve the congregation in baptism so that they are aware of the roles they play in persons' lives—as teachers, guides, and mentors. The congregation holds this time as holy and, as a result, feels connection with the whole, wider, church family." — *Kathleen Morgan, interim pastor, Northshore United Church of Christ, Woodinville, Washington*

GOD'S WORLD MATTERS

Connecting Sacraments with the Stuff of Life

In the sacraments, ordinary stuff of life conveys the presence of Christ to the world. Blessed through water, can we ever again simply take God's gift of water for granted? Fed with the bread of Christ, we are filled and transformed. Can we forget those who go without water and bread? God calls us to be stewards of the common stuff. In gratitude, blessed through the sacraments, we are called to share water and bread with the world.

Discover how the UCC is doing its part to raise justice issues surrounding the immediate and future availability of water throughout the world. Most vulnerable to the depletion are those on the margins, the poor, and the powerless. One special effort was the 2006 UCC production of the DVD *Troubled Waters*. The documentary presents the magnitude of this global concern. (Visit online at www.troubled watersdoc.com.) Thankful for God's goodness at baptism and the table, how do we work for adequate water and bread for those who suffer from little?

NOTES

1. See additional resources on baptism and Holy Communion in the United Church of Christ by visiting online www.ucc.org/worship/baptism/ and www.ucc.org/worship/communion/.

2. *Baptism, Eucharist and Ministry* (Geneva: World Council of Churches, 1982). Visit online at www.oikoumene.org/?id=2638.

3. *Worshiping into God's Future: Summary and Strategies 2005* (Cleveland: Worship & Education Ministry Team, Local Church Ministries, 2005). Visit online at www.ucc.org/worship/worshiping-into-gods-future/.

4. "Prayer for Baptism" in the order for Baptism, *Book of Worship: United Church of Christ,* reprint (Cleveland: Worship & Education Ministry Team, Local Church Ministries, 2002), 141.

You are invited to both the joy and responsibility of discipleship.

Imagine that a new world is possible.

5 we thank God by working for a just and loving world

WHAT MATTERS TO YOU

Every day you are surrounded by world news. Headlines stream across our consciousness through newspapers, television, radio, web, blogs, and cellular phones. As never before, we have access to information about millions of people with whom we share the planet. We know something of their world, their hopes and despair. It's tough to keep the world at a distance, especially as people of faith and followers of Christ. How does this wider world intersect with your own? The United Church of Christ seeks to provide a bridge between our private worlds and a wider world—linking you to God's great work of justice and love.

- In what ways do you typically express thanks to God?
- Recently, what local or global situation especially concerns you?
- In gratitude to God, how might you feel led to respond to that concern?

WHAT MATTERS TO US

"To believe is to care. To care is to do." Several years ago, this slogan was printed on bumper stickers to describe the United Church of Christ. Critics found the slogan lacking because it didn't mention God at all. For others close to the heart of the UCC, they knew God is at the heart of, and all wrapped up in, our caring and doing.

God creates. God loves. God's hope for all that God made is one of a peaceable realm of love and justice. As we are filled with gratitude for all God's good gifts, God's hope is our hope. Our hope connects with God's hope. We share in both God's vision and work for the entire world.

The Bible describes this vision in a variety of ways that includes paradise (Isaiah 11:6–9) and a peaceable realm (Isaiah 2:2–4), a great banquet (Luke 14:15–24), and a new heaven and earth (Revelation 21:1–5). We see it in God's delivery of those from slavery and hear it in the justice-loving voices of prophets. We especially see it in Jesus. In him, the realm of God drew near (Luke 17:20–21). He taught about it, proclaimed it in prophetic stances, and lived it through offering his life for others. We glimpse God's realm even now, and look for the fulfillment of God's love and justice in the future.

Look around and it doesn't take long to discover, however, that the vision isn't fully realized. We see a world where violence, discrimination, and hunger are weapons of greed and fear. We notice those who are ignored are often victims of other's self-interest—left in poverty with little hope. We wonder how long the world, our environmental home, can take the stress and depletion of human want. We scratch our heads in amazement that nations war against nations and religions war against religions—destroying the lives of the world's children.

Yet God's vision breaks through in the bold witness of God's people. By God's grace, we extend our hands to others through generous acts of compassion, service, and advocacy. We reach across cultural, racial, and religious divides, reconciling ourselves to one another. In solidarity with those who are most vulnerable in our world, we do justice. God comes in moments of healing, peace, and deliverance.

The UCC connects caring and acting, gratitude and giving, peace and justice, service and advocacy in a life of prayer and justice. At times, we are even called to go against the grain of conventional norms to root out injustice. We just don't usually settle for things to merrily roll along when our world is hurting.

We follow Christ's lead and seek to address a broad range of concerns. In 1959, soon after the founding of the UCC, we first outlined the broad arena of global concerns in the "Call to Christian Action in Society."[1] We identified settings that God calls us to address—the world of nations, the American culture, race relations, and political life. See also "Our History Matters," page 63, to discover other past key moments in our commitment to justice and love.

Today, we continue to encourage both individuals and congregations to respond to God's call to justice around numerous issues.[2] We address issues of civil and human rights, as well as economic and racial justice. We are leaders in uncovering ways in which environmental policies are connected with racism and poverty. We advocate on behalf of children's education and health care. We have spoken for marriage and employment equality for lesbian, gay, and bisexual citizens. Our efforts extend beyond any one local setting to the world where we work for God's peace, environmental justice, and healing in the midst of disease and hunger.

Because of God's liberating love, we imagine that another world is possible. We are called to participate in God's reign, even now, of love and justice.

- What connections do you and your congregation directly have with persons who suffer injustice and violence, locally and globally?

- What injustices and conflicts, locally and globally, weigh heavily upon the heart of your congregation? What is God saying to you about those concerns?

PRAYER MATTERS

The Examen ▪ *Holding the Day before God*

Together, both prayer and action draw us deeply to God and to others. Together they form a path toward fulfilling Jesus' call to "love God" and "love neighbor" (Mark 12:28–34). At the end of your day, when your head's about to hit the pillow, enter a way of praying that recalls God and neighbor. The "examen" is a spiritual practice that holds your day before God.

Aware of God's presence, enter into a time of prayer. Imagine, recall, or glance at the happenings of your day. Be still and aware of what arises. What makes you grateful? Where was God in the day for you? Who comes to your mind? What situations—including local and global situations—arise? When did you do justice, extend mercy? What feels like a missed opportunity? For whom do you feel called to continue to pray for? What lingers in your heart that you need to pray for or do something about? Hold all this before God, offer yourself to God's care, and rest.

BIBLE MATTERS

Micah 6:6–8 ▪ *What Does God Require?*

Begin exploring Micah 6:6–8 through prayer, by asking God, "Merciful and Just God, what do you require of me, of us?" Spend a few moments in silence.

Read Micah 6:6—8 aloud slowly. Pause after the first reading, and then read again.

Perhaps sing a version of the passage if you are familiar with the popular song "What Does the Lord Require of You?" or "Every Step of the Way."[3]

Consider: Verses 1 to 5 in the sixth chapter of Micah set the context for the more popular portion in 6:6–8. First, the earlier verses briefly recall the story of God's delivering the Hebrews from slavery—reminding God's people that they were recipients of God's mercy and justice. The well-known Bible snippet then takes the form of Israel's early worship practice. As people entered the temple, priests asked a question to prepare them for worship. Micah uses the same approach to get to the heart of what God desires. Normally, in worship, the answer focused on such worship practices as making burnt or sacrificial offerings. Here in Micah, however, the answer to what God requires names doing justice and loving mercy.

Prayerfully reflect: Pray again, "Merciful and Just God, what do you require of me, of us?" Wait in silence. What seems to come to your heart or mind? Or reflect on a question such as "How do I express thanks to God for the ways God shows mercy and justice to me?" or "What is God asking of me or my congregation at this time?"

PEOPLE MATTER

"When we experience God's great love for us, we surely want to pass it on to help speed God's love around the globe—making the world a more caring place!" —*Cally Rogers-Witte, executive minister, Wider Church Ministries, UCC, Cleveland, Ohio*

"We have to move from charity to justice by addressing systematic issues of jobs, health care, and safety" —*Marilyn Pagán-Banks, copastor, Good News Community Church UCC, Chicago, Ilinois, acknowledging how the significant ministry of a soup kitchen led the congregation to political and social advocacy*

"When your voice is not popular, then that may be the exact sign that God needs you to speak. We're each to be the best for what God has called us. We're not called to be popular or successful. Don't forsake the work of God's justice." —*Dennis Apuan, director of Pikes Peak Justice and Peace Commission, member of First Congregational UCC, Colorado Springs, Colorado)*

GOD'S WORLD MATTERS

Peace That Joins Protest to Prayer

During the UCC's 2007 General Synod, many leaders in the denomination published a pastoral letter about the war in Iraq calling for the end of violence and the beginning of a lasting peace. Between that June and the following October, more than sixty-three thousand letters from members of the UCC and their friends were collected supporting the petition for peace.[4] On October 10, 2007, the president of the church, John Thomas, and executive minister for justice-witness ministries, Linda Jaramillo, presented the letters to congressional leaders in Washington, D.C., and were later arrested for refusing to leave a no-protest zone near the White House. In what ways do you and your congregation take bold steps for your faith? How do you express God's call to love and justice?

NOTES

1. "Call to Christian Action in Society," *The Living Theological Heritage*, vol. 7, eds. Frederick R. Trost and Barbara Brown Zikmund (Cleveland: Pilgrim Press, 2005), Doc. 15, 81–85.

2. For information about numerous justice issues and opportunities, visit www.ucc.org/justice/issues/.html. For information on international issues and opportunities, visit www.globalministries.org.

3. "Every Step of the Way" is available online at www.ucc.org/assets/pdfs/acc7 .pdf.

4. For information about the United Church of Christ's efforts in peacemaking visit www.ucc.org/justice/peacemaking/.

Look, listen all around.
God's trying to tell us something.

There is yet more light and truth to
break forth from God's Holy Word.

6 we listen for the still-speaking God

WHAT MATTERS TO YOU

A colorful sunset, the birth of a child, or the embrace of a lifelong lover; an astonishing melody, a long-awaited peace, the taste of a holy meal, or a victory for human rights—does God have anything to do with these remarkable happenings? It's not always easy to determine the voice of God, but the United Church of Christ is bold to say, "God speaks, God speaks to us today!" God is even trying to tell you something.

- What sound or voice brings you great joy?
- What sound or voice do you long to hear?
- What are sounds or voices of God?
- What are the sounds of God's realm breaking through?

WHAT MATTERS TO US

If you think God's not finished with you yet, guess what? God's not even finished with God yet. God isn't finished with you, or finished with the church or our world, or even letting us know even more about God's own compassion, justice, hope, and truth. If you are open, if you listen carefully, you'll discover what God is saying to this generation at this time in history. There's more good news to be heard!

This understanding of God's "revelation" is a central aspect of UCC faith. We believe that God was revealed in the past, but also in the present and the future. In the Bible, God was known through covenants with people and nations, through prophets and teachers, through conflicts and commandments, in visions and songs, and through the followers of Jesus and the church. God acted profoundly in the life and ministry, even in the death, of Christ. On Easter, God declared in the resurrection of Jesus Christ, "I'll never, never stop speaking. Alleluia!" The resurrection assures us that God will never desert us. Even beyond death, God speaks life eternal. Throughout history, in moments of compassion, justice, and peace, in our worship, sacraments, prayer, seeking, action, and silence, God continues to speak.

In the UCC, the preamble of our Constitution (see page 75) reminds us that we are called "in each generation to make this faith our own." A recent UCC slogan conveys the call in another way: "Our faith is over 2000 years old. Our thinking is not." Now, we join with those who came before us in discerning God's voice for our own time.

You are encouraged to discover God speaking through the Bible. We believe we are called to be attentive to God's Word.[1] The Word we discover there, however, is not frozen in time. "Indeed, the word of God is living and active" (Hebrews 4:12). If you explore the Bible and move from book to book, you may discover that God is revealed in different ways, sometimes even seemingly contradictory ways. At distinct moments in biblical history, God speaks in new ways about God's unchanging intent of love, justice, deliverance, community, reconciliation, and peace.

As early in our history as our Pilgrim predecessors, we have talked about how God continues to shed "more light and truth" in our world. (See "Our History Matters," page 68, about this phrase.) In a similar way, we are not limited by past understandings of scripture, but we seek new insights and help for living the faith today. God is not finished with us yet.

In 1975, Oliver Powell stated, "Clearly the stance of the United Church is toward the world. All its doors and windows are open onto it. The church believes that God loves the world as much as [God] loves the church. . . ."[2] Because our doors and windows are open, we listen for God in a variety of places out in the world: in the arts, in political struggles, in the sciences, in media, in education, and especially in voices of those who are often ignored.

For example, we are not a people who simply dismiss reason and science as an enemy of faith. We affirm that God, indeed, may work through the sciences. We have joined with other denominations who present evolution in a way that is not in opposition to faith, but rather considers science as another way of appreciating the beauty and complexity of God's creation.

We also cherish the arts. In 1977, at our 11th General Synod, we expressed how God speaks through the arts as prophetic and effective channels of God's judgment and grace. We said that when "we are drawn into a work of art, we experience its transforming power; the arts open us to new ways of understanding both personal and public life and give us insight and energy to act in love and justice for the sake of the Holy."[3]

Today, God is especially speaking through a beautiful diversity of voices. God continues to form us through new people among us, offering a multicultural mosaic that reflects all of creation. We also hear God's voice in public policy that advocates for those who are poor, hungry, or most vulnerable in our society.

We celebrate our common ground, while honoring our differences. We embody Saint Augustine's ancient dictum: "In essentials, unity; in nonessentials, diversity; in all things, charity." In covenant with one another, we prayerfully seek together as the church, the body of Christ, to discern God's voice in the midst of so many voices. We are aware, at the same time, that God's voice may come in a lone voice, crying out in a world that does not listen.

Even without words at all, often as we wait in silence, we know God still comes.

- When have you experienced a conflict between one person who believes God says one thing regarding a concern and another who believes God says something else about the concern? How do you discern God's voice?
- Where do you hear or see God most frequently?
- How is God nudging, comforting, or challenging you or your congregation lately?

PRAYER MATTERS

A Breath Prayer ▪ *Just Listening for God*

So often we think of prayer as talking to God, telling God what we're grateful for, what we're sorry for, or what we hope for. Prayer is far more than talking; it's a time of waiting, resting, and listening for God. Breath prayer is a prayerful practice that may open you more to listening and less to talking.

Set aside a time for prayer as little as three minutes or so to as much as twenty minutes. You might even use a kitchen timer to keep track of your time apart.

Sit comfortably, close your eyes, and become aware of your breathing. Breathe deeply. Become aware that you are in the living presence of God and of your intent to be open to God in the silence. Continue to rhythmically, gently breathe in and out. Be aware with each breath that you are waiting and resting in God.

When thoughts or images arise, acknowledge them for a second and then release them to God, returning to simply focusing on your breathing.

At the conclusion of the time, thank God for the time. Upon opening your eyes, consider how you experienced God in the time.

BIBLE MATTERS

Psalm 46:1–10 ▪ *Be Still and Know God*

Spend some time in silence. Be aware of God's presence as you open yourself to the very real possibility that God may reveal a healing or challenging word to you or your community. Trust in God's presence.

Read Psalm 46:1–10 aloud. Consider reading the version of the psalm found in *The New Century Hymnal*, page 652, or from *The New Century Psalter*, page 81.[4]

Identify what comes to mind and heart. Psalm 46 is full of imagery and includes a wide range of emotions and insights. What particular words or images linger after hearing the reading? What disturbs you, comforts you, surprises you? What do you wonder about?

Consider: Psalm 46 emphasizes God who speaks justly to ancient Israel and to creation, other nations, and, finally, in the silence of the assembly gathered for worship. In this view, although God is revealed in particular places as "the city of God," God is not dependent on a particular place. God's very self is the only true refuge. In silence, the faithful know God but still are open to God's continuing mysterious revelation. After these reflections, rest in God.

Open to God's calling: Slowly read Psalm 46:1–10 one more time. Consider how God might touch you in both comforting and challenging ways. Perhaps God is calling you to do something in particular. Perhaps God wants you to change in some way. Perhaps God is leading you to speak or act with particular people and situations.

Continue your prayer by thanking God for God's guidance and for being "a refuge" and a "living Word." Ask God to continue to form you and your community through the scripture. Then, be still; rest in the presence of God.

PEOPLE MATTER

"Open your heart in the morning and in the evening. We must always remember to open our hearts to God's message because God is not finished with us yet. Oh no, God is still speaking and it's time for us to start listening." —*Marcus Lewis, young adult member of the UCC and keynote speaker at National Youth Event 2004, Knoxville, Tennessee*

"To make our faith our own is a responsibility of each generation. . . . God's still speaking." —*Edith A. Guffey, associate general minister of the UCC, Office of General Ministries, UCC, Cleveland, Ohio*

"My God is a creating God, and, by God, I'm going to make sure my church remains creative. . . . Anyone who says you can't 'teach an old dog new tricks' must not be a member of UCC. Change is good, and I'm still as in love with my church as I ever was." —*Pete Koprowski, beloved older member of Pilgrim Congregational UCC, Cleveland, Ohio*

GOD'S WORLD MATTERS

God Still Speaks ▪ *Criminal Justice*

As people of the still-speaking God, the UCC affirms the ways that God still moves through our world—opening new possibilities, bringing healing, reconciling places of violence and despair. God points to places like our criminal justice system, which continues to emphasize a response of revenge for wrongful acts. It takes a powerful witness to a still-speaking God to try to see a new way. Among those seeking new ways are many working to abolish the death penalty in the United States.

The United States remains one of only a handful of nations to administer the death penalty in the context of a criminal justice system that is not always just, but often taints justice with the bias of class and race. The death penalty closes off the possibility of redemption and reconciliation; it usurps the word of the still-speaking God.

Among those working for the abolition of the death penalty are members of a group called Murder Victim Families for Reconciliation (visit online at www.mvfr.org). The group includes people who experienced the loss of a loved one through the violent act of another, yet wish to see the cycle of violence end. To learn more about UCC efforts, visit online at www.ucc.org/justice/criminal-justice.

NOTES

1. In 1993, the General Synod of the UCC advocated the commitment to be a church attentive to the Word in the twenty-first century. Visit online www.ucc.org /beliefs/toward-the-21st-century.html.

2. "The UCC: A Beautiful, Heady, Exasperating Mix," *The Living Theological Heritage*, vol. 7, eds. Frederick R. Trost and Barbara Brown Zikmund (Cleveland: Pilgrim Press, 2005), Doc. 53, 301–5.

3. "Resolution on the Church and the Arts," *The Living Theological Heritage*, vol. 7, eds. Frederick R. Trost and Barbara Brown Zikmund (Cleveland: Pilgrim Press, 2005), Doc. 50, 275.

4. *The New Century Hymnal* (Cleveland: Pilgrim Press, 1995) and *The New Century Psalter* (Cleveland: Pilgrim Press, 1999).

"Faith is only real when it's shaped out of every generation's struggle."

— Valerie Russell[1]

7 our history matters

What matters to you today is profoundly shaped by what has mattered in the past. What are the powerful influences—both times and people, both wonderful and troubling—that make up who you are? What has God been doing with you since your first breath?

What matters to us in the UCC today is also seen in the defining moments of our past. In 2007, the United Church of Christ turned fifty years old or, as the quip declared, "fifty years bold!" Formed in 1957, we point to a heritage, however, that goes much further back.[2]

We see clues about what matters to us from the early New Testament church through the Protestant Reformation of the sixteenth and seventeenth centuries. We especially find ourselves in the distinctive histories that united to form us in the twentieth century: the German Evangelical and Reformed traditions as well as those of Congregational and Christian churches.[3] Since becoming the UCC, our more recent history accents a great diversity of people and opportunities. Although such diversity was present in the past and has always formed us, it often, however, was a hidden history.[4]

In this chapter, discover twenty-one snippets drawn from the stories of our past—some familiar, some hidden. These sketches do not detail a chronological history of who we are. Instead, they attempt to exemplify our vital themes. Most of them could easily embody more than any one theme. As you look at a story, you can see how themes of our faith—Christ, hospitality, covenant, unity, sacrament, justice, and revelation—dynamically interact with each other to express who and what has shaped us today.

Allow the stories to stir you to explore your own congregation's past. How has your local church embodied these themes over the years? What are the defining moments; who are the inspiring people who shaped your congregation? At what moments in your congregation's life can you say, "Yes, God was present then!" If you're new to your congregation, invite someone to tell you these stories.

Whenever you first entered the UCC, you entered our history. Now, you are called to prayerfully and boldly live a faith that will both create memories of who we have been and shape the future of who we will be. God spoke in the past and still speaks. God invites you into a history that matters, our living history.

WE ARE PEOPLE OF GOD'S EXTRAVAGANT WELCOME

What moments in our past exemplify bold hospitality, inclusiveness, and diversity?

Aloha, Who Welcomes Whom?

You would think Congregational missionaries headed for Hawaii in 1819 would extend Christ's welcome to the Native Hawaiians. History, however, reveals that the adventure was as much about extending New England culture as it was extending Christ's welcome. (James

Michener's popular novel *Hawaii*, as well as a movie based on the book, depicts this tension.) Instead, it seems that it was the "Aloha" of Native Hawaiians that demonstrated God's hospitality in a surprising way.

One of the Hawaiians was Malo. He was highly regarded by the people of the island for his intimate love of tradition, including his particular mastery of the hula. When he moved to Maui in 1823, he welcomed the missionary William Richard and learned how to read and write English. He eventually converted, was baptized, and took the name "David."

Malo extended Christ's welcome to his own people as well by translating the gospel of Matthew into Hawaiian. In time, however, he grew discouraged and spoke against missionary efforts that "tended to diminish the people of the islands." He saw many of these conditions as fallout of U.S. culture: disease, inept leadership, and weakness in traditional Hawaiian culture.[5]

Malo became increasingly involved in a larger struggle with U.S. interests when native Hawaiian lands were confiscated for commercial use. He joined other Hawaiians in protesting such action. Yes, David Malo expressed an extravagant welcome to the missionaries, yet he showed an even bolder welcome in extending God's aloha—love, justice and peace—to those who were victims of injustice.

Four-year-old Lee, Finally Welcomed

In 1853, the slave woman Miriam refused to let her children be taken from her and also sold into slavery. She grabbed up her children and grandchildren—including four-year-old Lee Howard Dobbins—and traveled the "underground railroad." Not an actual train track, this railroad was a network of people working to assist fugitive slaves, just like her and her children.

By the time they arrived in Oberlin, Ohio, the journey had been especially difficult for Lee Howard. He was extremely ill. Miriam was concerned both for Lee Howard's health and about how long it might take for him to recover. Certain the angry master was not far behind them, she was troubled for the safety of all the children. A family in Oberlin came to Miriam's aid and welcomed Lee, promising to care for him. Hoping for Lee to soon follow them, Miriam and the other children continued, escaping to Canada. A week later, however, Lee Howard died.

The doors of the Congregational church in Oberlin opened for Lee Howard's funeral. The place was filled with the entire community—an incredible outpouring of grief for the child and the violence that slavery ravaged on all God's children. The pastor stirred the congregation with these words:

> Erect a monument to the memory of the little slave boy,
> bearing the inscription, *"Resurgam* [Rise again]":
> and believe that as certainly as this little one shall rise again,
> so surely it is written on the institution of slavery, "it shall fall."
> While you meditate, give thanks that our ancestors in the faith
>   stood firmly
> against the false claims of culture and acted out the Gospel
>   through defiant deeds of love.
> Pray for the strength to do the same today . . .
> and do not be afraid to weep.[6]

Yes, Virginia, There Is Compassion. Thanks to You!

When Virginia Kreyer talked about growing up with cerebral palsy, a condition that disorders body, muscle, and speech coordination, she was especially grateful to her mother. Without her mother, she said, "I would not have been able to be the woman I have become." The woman who Virginia has become is a rare human being whose faith and witness has inspired the UCC to extend an extravagant welcome. Her welcome embraces all people, but especially those with disabilities.

Ordained in 1952, Kreyer has served as a chaplain, inspiring and caring for others with cerebral palsy. She has also taken ground-breaking actions on behalf of others with disabilities in both the UCC and society. For so long she saw little support by the church for persons with disabilities. In 1976, however, she spoke out at a New York UCC conference meeting when a kind visitor from Japan observed that he hadn't seen one person with disabilities. Virginia went to the nearest microphone and called for a resolution to the next UCC national Synod that would recognize and encourage pastoral care for persons with disabilities.

At the following Synod while worshiping in the Washington National Cathedral, people with disabilities led a parade with banners. Virginia and her friend, Harold Wilke, spoke, and it resulted in Synod action calling for work with persons with disabilities becoming a priority for the UCC.[7] God embraced Virginia. Virginia continues to welcome others as God has welcomed her.

WE BELONG TO CHRIST

When, in our history, have we embodied the commitment to belonging to Christ?

What's a Catechism and What Does It Have to Do with Anything?

In 1562, in Germany, Lutheran and Reformed churches fought and demanded loyalty to particular beliefs.[8] Theologians argued with one another. Bitter fights arose particularly in Heidelberg. The prince, Frederick III, concerned for peace to end the hostility, called for order and a new catechism.

Some folks think of a catechism as a bunch of questions and answers that people have to memorize to make everyone of one mind. Catechisms can, however, clarify things and sometimes bring people together in faith. Frederick's catechism sought to draw people together and offered faith in Christ as a way of healing.

The first question of this catechism was "What is your only comfort, in life and in death?" To which the response began: "That I belong—body and soul, in life and in death—not to myself, but to my faithful Savior, Jesus Christ . . ."[9] This answer suggested that we don't belong to the opinion of a particular theologian or national creed; we don't even belong to our own beliefs, but we belong to Jesus Christ.

Brave Belonging

Today, forty congregations with direct historical ties to the Hungarian Reformed Church are part of the United Church of Christ. Their story includes an account of brave belonging. In 1674, Hungarian Reformed ministers were among forty-two Protestants who were sold as galley slaves and chained to oars on trade ships in the Adriatic Sea. Hungarian Protestants, especially the poor, suffered intense persecution in the midst of a dominant Catholic majority that battled against the rise of the broader Protestant movement in Europe. These forty-two refused to recant their faith.[10]

Károly Jeszensky wrote the "Hymn of the Hungarian Galley Slaves," or "Lift Your Heads, O Martyrs, Weeping," based on original words of Pauli Joachim, who experienced the persecution. The hymn expresses the devotion to Christ of those persecuted, their conviction about belonging to Christ, and Christ's abiding care for those who belong to God. The closing words of the hymn powerfully affirm that relationship: "You are God's own people; surely God will fold God's own securely." This is the second verse of the hymn that became an anthem of liberation for Hungarian Protestants:

> Though the storms may rage and roil
> o'er the vast and fearful sea,
> Though you cry with wretched toil,
> "O my Savior, rescue me!"
> Though it seems that God does sleep,
> hope and trust in God still keep;
> Calm your hearts though they be quaking,
> God is faithful, none forsaking.[11]

What a Difference Christ Makes

"We Belong to Christ" was affirmed as well on the frontier of the United States. During the late eighteenth and early nineteenth centuries, many people were swept up in an enthusiastic faith in Christ that eventually led to the forming of the Christian Church.[12] The heartfelt faith appealed to both European immigrants and former African slaves invited into the revival.

Many of these people left other churches, insisting on a new way of believing and being the church. They wanted a less hierarchical way of governing and less reliance on the authority of creeds. Their faith was full of feeling. Although not anti-intellectual, they emphasized direct experience *with* Christ as much as belief *about* Christ. This experience would lead to a church where all, clergy and laity, were understood as radically equal. They characterized their faith in six "Principles of the Christian Church."[13]

"Christ as the sole head of the Church" was the first among the six principles. The phrase suggested that when members tried to resolve conflicts or figure out issues, they prayed for Christ's guidance and listened to one another rather than demanded particular tests or obeyed only one authoritative voice.[14] The conviction also led to other principles. For example, Christian character—the way you live your life—

was as important as any belief. And because Christ is the head of the church, all who confess Christ, even with their differences, are still one in Christ. The church is one.

Claiming Christ from the Start

 In 1957, when the UCC was formed, and again in 1960, when our constitution was adopted, we drew upon and were inspired by our commitment to Christ. It is evident both in naming our newly formed denomination the United Church of Christ and in the preamble of our constitution.[15] The second paragraph of the preamble states: "The United Church of Christ acknowledges as its sole Head, Jesus Christ, Son of God and Savior. It acknowledges as kindred in Christ all who share in this confession." (Read the entire preamble on page 75). Belonging to Christ has shaped both our theological identity and how we relate to all God's children.

WE ARE A PEOPLE OF COVENANT, A UNITED AND UNITING CHURCH

What are some of the moments in our past when we exemplified a covenant way of life and a commitment to unity?

Salem: A Covenant of Peace?

As for covenants, our English forebearers loved to make them. The Pilgrims had the Mayflower Compact.[16] And in 1629, a group of Puritans sailed across the Atlantic to a fishing village called Naumkeag, Massachusetts, and established another covenant. The Salem covenant joined the settlers' personal, church, and public lives—calling on them to walk together in God's holy ways. The locals picked up on their holy vision, and, together, they renamed the village Salem, meaning "peace." Their old-English covenant sounded like this:

We covenant with the Lord
and one with an other
and doe bynd our selves in the presence of God,
to walke together in all his waies, according as he is pleased
to reveale himself unto us
in his blessed word of truth.[17]

Clergy from the two churches process in Cleveland, Ohio,
celebrating the merger, 1957.
(UCC Archives, United Church of Christ, Cleveland, Ohio)

When the Salem congregation needed assistance, they reached
out to the Plymouth colony of Pilgrims. The Pilgrims extended their
fellowship to the church at Salem. Thus began covenantal relationships between our congregations. Salem, however, wasn't always so
peaceful. There were days of terror. In 1692, Salem convicted and
executed nineteen persons as witches. Church members were
among the accusers, the defenders, and the executed. The covenant
shook.

Today, members of one of the three congregations with direct links
to the original First Church of Salem continue to declare the
covenant, at least four times a year, in fresh language. One of those
congregations, Tabernacle Congregational Church UCC, continues a
covenantal way of life.

The Big Covenant of 1957

From informal letters and conversations beginning in 1937, clergy
from the Congregational Christian Churches of the United States and

the Evangelical Reformed Church explored their faith and work.[18] In spite of different ethnic origins and ways of governing their church life, they discovered "a strong unity of thought and mind." In 1942, the denominations got serious about that discovery and formed a joint committee on union. The *Christian Century* magazine in October of that year described the two churches' effort: "It is a significant and heartening fact that these two churches which have had a taste of union want more of it! They are not content to be merely united churches, but wish to be uniting churches."[19]

Almost twenty years later, after conversations, negotiations, prayers, reams of paper, writing a "Basis of Union," and then still more conversations and court cases, the churches united.[20] On June 25, 1957, the United Church of Christ was formed in Cleveland, Ohio. Among the jubilant words, music, and prayers, Gerhard W. Grauer prayed to God: "We covenant together, but we cannot create, we cannot unite, we cannot constitute a United Church of Christ. What we propose, do Thou perform."[21]

Walk-out—A Hispanic Prophetic Call to Covenant

Worship and witness of local Hispanic congregations had been vital for years. In 1987, however, many Hispanics were weary and frustrated with the broader UCC's "neglectful response to the needs of Hispanics."[22] Our covenant weakened.

That year, at the General Synod in Ames, Iowa, a Mexican American layperson from New York City, Abraham Reyes, called Synod to be a covenant people. He proposed a resolution that called for greater involvement of the Hispanic community in national leadership, ministries, and resource development. In his statement, he concluded: "Our soul is hurting and our hearts are broken! It is therefore, with a profound sense of corporate loss, that we must leave you now! We will return to hear your response to our claim for justice." (At that point the Hispanic delegation walked out of the Synod auditorium.)

At a later session of Synod, Reyes and Avery Post, president of the UCC, walked together, along with members of the Hispanic council, into the auditorium to a standing ovation and song. Post reported "a healing suggestion for us all" along with a plan for more inclusive leadership in the broader church. Reyes responded: "We come back to you with faith, and a spirit of reconciliation, to call each other to do our mission. It isn't my mission, it isn't the Hispanics' mission, nor your mission; it's God's mission. A time to build, a time to heal."

WE ARE ONE AT BAPTISM AND AT THE TABLE

In our past, when have we expressed the significance of baptism and Holy Communion?

God Troubles the Water—Radical Baptism

Today, seeing an infant baptized is a lovely event. Even when the baby cries from chilly water, "ooohs" and "ahhs" from the congregation fill the sanctuary. Our history, however, is filled with stories, not so sweet, of how radical, even politically world-shaking, baptism can be.

Baptism for enslaved people in colonial and antebellum America was a radical event. The meaning of baptism was debated by those in power. Should slaves be baptized? Does being baptized in Christ make one free in this world as well as the next? The answer by many in power was "no." As early as 1639, Maryland was the first colony to specifically state that baptism as a Christian did not make a slave free.

In 1883, following the emancipation of slaves, Frederick Douglass, the famous orator, teacher, and former slave, pointed to how baptism challenged the institution of slavery. At the Congregational Church in Washington, D.C., Douglass declared: "Baptism was then a vital and commanding question, one with which moral and intellectual giants of the day were required to grapple. . . . When a heathen ceased to be a heathen and became a Christian, he could no longer be held as a slave."[23] In spite of arguments against the baptism of those enslaved, Christ led folk to the water. "God troubled the waters."

Worship Wars, Warring Words

Can you imagine debating for over three decades about a book of worship and what to include in it? It's part of our history from about 1847 to 1887. The German Reformed Church, one of our predecessor denominations, struggled to discern the meaning of the sacraments as it worshiped in the United States during a time bridging the frontier and modern society.[24]

The church formed a committee to offer a book of worship that would faithfully provide Reformed liturgies to congregations. Over time a debate developed that particularly focused around the critical thinking of two Pennsylvania pastor-professors, John William Nevin and John H. A. Bomberger.

Nevin, who represented the emerging Mercersburg Theology, called on the church to reincorporate the tradition, creeds, and practices of the ancient church—especially a renewed commitment to the presence, the mystery, of Christ at Holy Communion.

Bomberger, at first a supporter of Nevin, finally rejected Nevin's emphasis on the ancient and "Catholic," and insisted on understandings that he felt more in keeping with the Reformation and also the popular revival movement of the day with its free-form worship

*John V. Nevin,
Mercersburg theologian.*
(UCC Archives, United Church of Christ, Cleveland, Ohio)

style. Bomberger's supporters, often known as "Old Reformed" or "The Ursinus School" (named after the school in southeastern Pennsylvania where the movement centered) met in Myerstown, Pennsylvania, in 1867 to clearly state their opposition to the seemingly growing support for Nevin's liturgy.

Throughout the debate, committees usually favored Nevin and his emphasis on the mystical power of sacraments. When the *Directory of Worship* was finally adopted in 1887, it offered the rich ancient sacramental tradition expressed by Nevin. It also, however, offered a variety of other resources and encouraged the use of free or extemporaneous prayers. Congregations were able to choose between options. "Mercersburg" and "Old Reformed" emerged together.

Although the debate was often polarizing and painful, the struggle encouraged congregations to examine understandings of baptism and Holy Communion and how they express the grace of God today in a contemporary context.

With What Words Will We Pray?

Where do the words come from that you hear and say at baptism or Holy Communion? In 1977, the eleventh General Synod of the UCC called on the church to craft words for a book of worship "using inclusive language." From 1979 until the 1986 publication of the *Book of Worship*, a committee of ten prayerfully discerned words faithful to tradition, committed to justice, and celebrating the presence and grace of God.[25]

This commitment was not a move toward often belittled political correctness. Rather it reflected a commitment to the expansiveness of God and to God's embrace of all. The commitment embraced language about men and women, but also language sensitive to race, abilities, and the goodness of creation. It also encouraged active participation of "total persons to the loving initiative of God"—suggesting ways of worship beyond speaking including embracing, touching, pouring, anointing, and singing. It was inclusive in another way, an ecumenical way. The *Book of Worship* reflected the liturgical renewal movement—an influence that also shaped worship in other denominations in common, yet ancient, forms.

Some traditional words remained and others were revised for both baptism and Holy Communion. In the baptism service, one hears about distinct ways God has called upon women. In the thanksgiving prayer for baptism, we recall "Jesus Christ, who was nurtured in the water of Mary's womb" and who "became living water to a woman at the Samaritan well." Rather then rehearsing the entire Apostles Creed, believers are asked three questions based on the traditional Trinity form. The questions both recall tradition and open up the possibility for fresh understandings of the Triune God.

Words for Holy Communion were also prayerfully considered. The invitation to Communion reflects the inclusive heart of the liturgy:

This is the joyful feast of the people of God.
Men and women, youth and children,
come from the east and the west,
from the north and the south,
and gather about Christ's table.[26]

The *Book of Worship* received both favorable and unfavorable reviews. Yet the eventual acceptance of the *Book of Worship* encouraged a continuing commitment to inclusive language especially evident in our 1995 hymnal, *The New Century Hymnal.*

WE THANK GOD BY WORKING FOR A JUST AND LOVING WORLD

When have we exemplified the UCC's profound commitment to working for God's justice and love?

Stop the Chains of Oppression

"Give us free! Give us free!" shouted Senge Pieh, a young Mende African man before the U.S. District Court in Hartford, Connecticut, in 1839.[27] Senge was one of many Africans imprisoned for a revolt aboard the Spanish ship *Amistad.* Captured as slaves in Sierre Leone, they fought against their captors and were later recaptured off the coast of New London, Connecticut. Their struggle for freedom became a rallying moment for the abolition movement in this country and set the direction for our church's future justice work.

The Amistad Committee was founded by abolitionists in Connecticut, including many prominent Congregationalists, to assist in the legal battles for release of the imprisoned Mendes. While they were in prison, congregations and teachers from Yale Divinity School also cared for the Mendes by teaching English, reading, and basics of the Christian faith. After two difficult trials and political opposition from President Martin Van Buren, their case was finally heard before the Supreme Court in 1841. The Amistad Committee persuaded former president John Quincy Adams to argue their case. They were acquitted and free!

The committee continued and raised funds to charter a ship for the Mendes to return home to Sierre Leone. They also formed the American Missionary Association (AMA) in 1846,

Senge Pieh
painted by Nathaniel Jocelyn.
New Haven Colony Historical Society.

which was a vital center of the abolitionist movement until the Civil War. The AMA made stands on behalf of racial justice, establishing more than five hundred schools and colleges for African Americans, founding congregations, and advocating for justice on behalf of Asian Americans and American Indians as well.

Two Worlds, One in Christ

At twenty-one years old, in 1864, Neesima Shimeta was a samurai, a member of Japan's royal military order. He was also drawn to an understanding of God that he had only read of in Chinese Christian missionary books. He wanted to know more.[28]

That year, he left Japan illegally for the United States. He boarded an American ship to Shanghai and persuaded the captain to take him to the United States. Stories of his journey include a port stop in Hong Kong, where Neesima sold his samurai sword to raise money to purchase a Chinese New Testament. Upon his arrival in Boston, the owner of the ship, Alpheus Hardy, adopted him. Hardy was a longtime member of American Board of Commissioners for Foreign Missions (a predecessor body to UCC Wider Church Ministries). In gratitude to Hardy, Neesima took the name Joseph Hardy Neesima.

With Hardy's help, Neesima attended Phillips Academy, Amherst College, and Andover Seminary. He was ordained in 1874 and became involved in the Japan mission of the American Board. The new emerging leaders of Japan were from the samurai class, as he had been, and Neesima desired Christianity to reach out to them and others through higher education.

In 1874, Neesima appealed to the American Board for their support of a Western-style Christian school in Japan. Initially he received minimal support. Once he returned to Japan and opened Doshisha School in 1875, however, the Board officially adopted the school as part of their own mission. The school was led by a purely Japanese administration, and soon thirty samurai entered the school and eventually graduated as Christian leaders. Even today, Doshisha University continues as a partner institution with the United Church of Christ.

Throughout his life, Neesima gave thanks to God through lifting up the possibilities of education for transforming God's world. He encouraged Christian higher education beyond that of pastors by advocating the establishment of a medical school and other significant fields of study. His broad understanding of evangelism blended with a love and hope for the social transformation of his homeland, Japan.

They're Not Nuns. They're Deaconesses!

St. Louis in the late 1880s was the new home of German immigrants, many with roots in the German Evangelical Church. Yet there was little medical care for many of those who were sick, poor, and aging within the city. At a meeting of the St. Louis Evangelical Pastor's Association, an Evangelical pastor asked, "Why can't we train the young women of our church to care for the poor and sick?" Soon, in 1889, the Evangelical Deaconess Society and the Evangelical Deaconess Home and Hospital were founded.

Katherine Haack, a trained nurse and widow of an Evangelical pastor, was the first deaconess to be consecrated and named the Sister Superior at the home. At a time when women were often silenced at church, women such as Haack were leaders in the administration and managed the home and hospital.

The Deaconess movement led to the establishment of some sixteen hospitals and institutions for health care and nurse training, as well as worldwide work. Through the years at the St. Louis Motherhouse, more than five hundred deaconess sisters were trained.

Led by deep faith, deaconesses demonstrated a life of both compassionate service and profound leadership. Their approach to nursing was loving and spiritual—and professional—similar to the nurture found at home. This contrasted with institutional care typical of that era when hospitals were used as a last resort for the dying. The deaconesses also modeled a bold new contribution by women, a holy calling, which would eventually lead to a more visible and increasing role of women in both church and society.[29]

Serenity Prayer and Justice

God, give us grace to accept with serenity the things
    that cannot be changed;
    courage to change the things that should be changed;
    and wisdom to distinguish the one from the other.[30]

Through the years, the popular "Serenity Prayer" has been embraced by thousands of persons recovering from addictions, prayed through the Alcoholic Anonymous fellowships. The prayer holds before God both the longing for wisdom and the courage to act needed by those who suffer addictions.

In the form above, the prayer was first crafted by Reinhold Niebuhr, an Evangelical and Reformed Church pastor and ethics professor. He first used the prayer as part of his sermon in the summer of 1943 at Union Church in Heath, Massachusetts.

Neibuhr's prayer was a prayer intended for a congregation's worship, but it was also a prayer rooted in a particular time of social and global upheaval. Faced with the evil and violence of a world war, Niebuhr asked the question: "What does the gospel mean in this situation?" Is war ever just in the face of overwhelming evil? Is pacifism always a faithful response? Does God call for acceptance or for change?[31]

Prayer and discernment of justice are linked. The prayer trusts that God still speaks. It calls on those who pray it to seek God's profound wisdom and then act.

Far from the Home They Love: Freedom to Worship

In 1987, Rosemary McCombs-Maxey was the first Native American woman, a member of the Muscogee Nation, to be ordained in the United Church of Christ. Her call to ministry has led her to link justice for Native Americans to justice for all God's people.[32]

Her commitment was apparent when she discovered that her own nation was negotiating with Hawaii to build a prison near her home in Oklahoma. She recalled the Trail of Tears and the unjust dislocation of more than twenty thousand of her own people to reservations. She linked that tragic injustice with the impending three-thousand-mile dislocation of Native Hawaiian prisoners from their home. McCombs-Maxey knew something needed to be done. So she reached out to ecumenical colleagues and the United Church of Christ for their help. Another Muscogee citizen joined her in addressing their national council to stop the negotiations.

She learned that Hawaii had already brought prisoners to the Diamondback Correctional Facility in Watonga, Oklahoma. She and others—including other native people from Hawaii, her own nation's citizens, and UCC clergy from the Kansas-Oklahoma Conference—became "unofficial" chaplains to the prisoners.

They discovered that prisoners were not allowed to practice their own indigenous religion. For over six years, prisoners attempted to get on the chapel schedule. Advocating for freedom to practice their faith resulted, at times, in "lock down." There were days when McCombs-Maxey and the others were not even allowed to visit the prisoners.

The official chaplain at the time said the native Hawaiian practices were pagan and that she would have "none of this other gibberish." She was critical of McCombs-Maxey and other UCC clergy for not converting the prisoners to the Christian faith. Rosemary responded to

Rosemary McCombs-Maxey
(UCC Archives, United Church of Christ, Cleveland, Ohio)

these judgments by saying: "Our brand of Christianity says to be respectful of their faith; we always honor the men in their religious tradition. That is where healing comes from."[33]

More than mere chaplain, McCombs-Maxey was an advocate for the prisoners' rights to practice their faith. She was joined by other UCC clergy as David Hansen, the conference minister for the Kansas-Oklahoma Conference, and Kekapa Lee, who was then head of the Association of Hawaiian Evangelical Churches. In 2003, even though the Indian Religious Freedom Act had existed since 1978, thirty-five prisoners filed a legal suit in order to practice their religion.

In 2005, this advocacy led to General Synod's passing the resolution for "Religious Freedom for Native Hawaiian Prisoners." That year, a judge finally acted to allow prisoners to celebrate the native Hawaiian religious rite of Makahiki, a rite celebrating peace and harmony. In the UCC, the work of God's justice demands courage, persistence, and prayer. We are called to join with others in moving beyond our own interests to those of all who suffer.

In Robert Weir's Embarkation of the Pilgrims, *John Robinson leads the Pilgrims in prayer before sailing to the New World. The painting hangs in the United States Capitol, Washington.*
(Architect of the Capitol,
http://www.aoc.gov/cc/photo-gallery/ptgs_rotunda.cfm)

WE LISTEN FOR THE STILL-SPEAKING GOD

When has the UCC powerfully proclaimed God's continuing presence and revelation?

More Light!

One of the often quoted sayings in the UCC goes something like this: "There's still more light and truth breaking through." The originator of the phrase was the Reverend John Robinson, pastor to the Pilgrims in Leiden, Holland, in 1620.[34] These familiar words were offered by Robinson to inspire the Pilgrims on the eve of their departure from the familiar to the New World ahead of them.

In a new and vital way, Robinson hoped that the Pilgrims would continue the Protestant Reformation that had swept Europe. Although he would not leave with them, Robinson called on them not to fear, but rather to be open to God's continuing revelation. God was present with them in their history. God was also ahead of them—in the New World, speaking in new ways. Robinson's actual words were:

We are now erelong to part asunder, and the Lord knoweth whether I shall live ever to see your faces more. But whether the Lord hath appointed it or not, I charge you before God and His blessed angels to follow me no farther than I have followed Christ. If God should reveal anything to you by any other instrument of His, be as ready to receive it as ever you were to receive any truth of my ministry; for I am very confident the Lord hath more truth and light yet to break forth out of His holy word.[35]

Can You Believe It? We Had a Heresy Trial about the Bible.

In 1880, by a vote of 47 to 9, Karl Otto, a Bible professor at Evangelical Seminary in Marthasville, Missouri, was "repudiated" for his method of teaching the Bible. That year at the General Conference of the Evangelical Synod, a committee investigated Otto's approach to the Bible and declared that he deviated from the doctrinal position of the church. They demanded that in the future Otto maintain "true doctrine."

Karl Otto was a bright scholar and pastor of German academic training. For him, God was speaking in a new way through study of the Bible that uncovered the original ancient context of scripture. The method was called "historical critical." He attempted to clearly distinguish what the Bible said in its original settings from the layers of church doctrine and tradition that had been heaped upon it. For him reason, science, and faith did not need to be pitted against each other.

Many pastors, however, were upset with Otto's critical approach. They preferred traditional or devotional understandings of passages. Otto defended himself, affirming both the authority of scripture and "liberty of conscience" that was part of the Evangelical's own 1848 confessional statement. Yet when the vote came up, it went against Otto, and he was dismissed from the synod. Otto went on to teach at Elmhurst College and to write both fiction and historical novels.

Over time, Otto's scholarship and inquiry was increasingly admired by people of the Evangelical and Reformed Church. The historian Carl Schneider stated that Otto was vindicated not only by posterity, but by his contemporaries who refused to deny open dialogue around biblical doctrine. At Otto's funeral, he was eulogized by Samuel D. Press, a student of Otto's. Press said that not only was Otto's theology centered in Christ, so was his life: "Through Otto's intellectual talents, God presented our church with one of his richest gifts. . . . Otto was an untiring searcher for the truth. . . . Otto had the courage to present his theological positions freely and openly, without concern for personal consequences."[36]

Karl Otto, in his mind and heart, knew the still-speaking God, and the still-speaking God spoke a challenging word through him.

Through the Airwaves, Listening for God's Voice

It was a long struggle. From 1953 to 1979, folk struggled to hear the voices of African Americans on the airwaves of Jackson, Mississippi. The United Church of Christ was instrumental throughout the battle.

When Jackson radio station WLBT went on the air in 1953, it had a policy not to allow any programming that dealt with racial integration. In 1955, Medgar Evers of the Mississippi NAACP first filed a

For more than twenty years, radio station WLBT, Jackson, Mississippi, was the sight of a struggle over the airwaves—to hear the voices of African Americans.
(UCC Archives, United Church of Christ, Cleveland, Ohio)

complaint about the policies of the station. The station continued through 1964 working against racial integration. In spite of a horrendous racist record, their license was repeatedly renewed.

In 1964, the UCC got on board to fight the good fight. The church initiated a study of the station's practices and then, in 1969, took the concern all the way to the United States Court of Appeals. Voices of African Americans were finally heard and the result was awarding a license to African American–controlled TV channel 3.

Everett Parker, the director of the UCC Office of Communications, called the decision "a resounding victory over deep-seated racial discrimination and a boon to minorities who have long been second-class citizens in television and radio. At last we have a black-controlled network affiliate. We hope this is the first step toward establishing a strong minority influence in network television."[37]

From the establishment of the first publishing press by the Pilgrims in 1621 to current battles with national television and cable networks about running the UCC's inclusive advertising, we have championed God's still-speaking voice through a wide range of media and communications.

NOTES

1. "Valerie Russell, UCC Executive, Dies at 55," February 24, 1997, Worldwide Faith News. Visit online at www.wfn.org/1997/02/msg00165.html.

2. *The Living Theological Heritage of the United Church of Christ, (LTH)*, series ed. Barbara Brown Zikmund (Cleveland: Pilgrim Press, 1995–2005). The seven-volume work presents documents, beginning in the first century CE and continuing through the twentieth century, that have shaped the theological identity of the UCC.

3. For additional information about our predecessor church traditions including the German Evangelical Movement, Congregationalism, the German Reformed Church, the Christian Churches, Evangelical and Reformed Church, and the Congregational Christian Churches, see the online resource, "A Short Course in the History of the UCC." Visit online www.ucc.org/about-us/short-course/.

4. Explore further *Hidden Histories in the United Church of Christ*, vols. 1 and 2, ed. Barbara Brown Zikmund (New York: United Church Press, 1984). Volume 1 available online at www.ucc.org/about-us/hidden-histories/.

5. David Malo, "On the Decrease of Population on the Hawaiian Islands," *LTH*, vol. 5, Doc. 24, 229–34.

6. Douglas S. Long, "Letter from First Church Minister regarding Underground Railroad Movement," September 22, 1993, Oberlin College Archives, Oberlin, OH.

7. Albert A. Herzog Jr., "A History of Disability Advocacy in the United Church of Christ," UCC Disabilities Network. Visit online at www.uccdm.org/2006/11/08 /a-history-of-disability-advocacy-in-the-united-church-of-christ/.

8. For more information, see "The German Reformed Church." Visit online at www.ucc.org/about-us/short-course/the-german-reformed-church.html.

9. "The Heidelberg Catechism," *LTH*, vol. 2, Doc. 2, 329. Also visit online at www.ucc.org/beliefs/heidelberg-catechism.html.

10. For more information, see John Butosi "The Calvin Synod: Hungarians in the United Church of Christ," *Hidden Histories*, vol. 1, 124–25.

11. "Lift Your Heads, O Martyrs, Weeping," *The New Century Hymnal* (Cleveland: Pilgrim Press, 1995), 445.

12. For more information, see "The Christian Churches." Visit online at www.ucc.org/about-us/short-course/the-christian-churches.html.

13. "Principles of the Christian Church," *Book of Worship*, reprint (Cleveland: Local Church Ministries, Worship and Education Ministry Team, 2002), 515. Also visit online at www.ucc.org/beliefs/principles-of-the-christian.html

14. *LTH*, vol. 4, 10–11.

15. "Basis of Union," *LTH*, vol. 6, Doc. 77, 583. Also visit online at www.ucc.org /beliefs/basis-of-union.html.

16. For more information, see "The Reformation in England" and "Congregationalism." Visit online at www.ucc.org/about-us/short-course/the-reformation-in -england.html and www.ucc.org/about-us/short-course/congregationalism.html.

17. "Salem Church Covenant," *Book of Worship*, reprint (Cleveland: Local Church Ministries, Worship and Education Ministry Team, 2002), 511.

18. For more information see "The Evangelical and Reformed Church" and "The Congregational Christian Churches." Visit online at www.ucc.org/about-us /short-course/the-evangelical-and-reformed.html and www.ucc.org/about-us/short -course/the-congregational-christian.html.

19. *LTH*, vol. 6, 505.

20. "Basis of Union," *LTH*, vol. 6, Doc. 77, 583. Also visit online at www.ucc.org /beliefs/basis-of-union.html.

21. *LTH*, vol. 6, Doc. 93, 744–46.

22. Abraham Reyes and Vilma Machín, "The Hispanic Walkout," *LTH*, vol. 7, Doc. 134, 731–34.

23. "Address by Honorable Frederick Douglass, Delivered in the Congregational Church Washington, D.C., April 16, 1883, on the Twenty-first Anniversary of Emancipation in the District of Columbia," pamphlet, 10–11. American Memory collection, series: Speech, Article, and Book File—A: Frederick Douglass, Dated; Frederick Douglass Papers, Library of Congress. Washington D.C., http://memory .loc.gov/cgi-bin/ampage?collId=mfd&fileName=24/24002/24002page.db&rec Num=5&itemLink=/ammem/doughtml/dougFolder5.html&linkText=7.

24. For more information see "The German Reformed Church." Visit online at www.ucc.org/about-us/short-course/the-german-reformed-church.html. See also

John C. Shetler, "The Ursinus School," *Hidden Histories*, vol. 1, 37–49, online at http://www.ucc.org/about-us/hidden-histories/the-ursinus-school-and-the.html. See also "The Myerstown Convention," Doc. 94, 565–74, and John Williamson Nevin, "The Church Movement: Seventh Article," Doc. 90, 544–49, LTH, vol. 4.

25. For more information, see "Order for Baptism" and "Service of Word and Sacrament I," *Book of Worship*, 129–44 and 31–54. See also Thomas Dipko, "Theological Guidelines that Informed," Doc. 34, 185–193, and Chalmer Coe, "Book of Worship: A Response," 194–199, LTH, Doc. 35, vol. 7.

26. *Book of Worship*, 44.

27. For more information, see Clara Merritt DeBoer, "Blacks and the American Missionary Association," *Hidden Histories*, vol. 1, 81–94, available online at www.ucc.org/about-us/hidden-histories/black-and-the-american.html. See also Arthur Abraham, "The Amistad Revolt: An Historical Legacy of Sierra Leone and the United States," online at http://usinfo.state.gov/products/pubs/amistad/.

28. Joseph Hardy Neesima, "Appeal to the Public," *LTH*, vol. 5, Doc. 45, 365–68, and Christian History Institute, "Neesima Shimeta: A Joseph for Japan." Visit online at http://chi.gospelcom.net/GLIMPSEF/Glimpses/glmps048.shtml.

29. Ruth W. Rasche, *The Deaconess Heritage* (St Louis: Deaconess Foundation, 1994), and Rasche, "The Deaconess Sisters: Pioneer Professional Women," *Hidden Histories*, vol. 1, 95–109. Also online at www.ucc.org/about-us/hidden-histories/the-deaconess-movement-in.html.

30. Reinhold Niebuhr, "The Serenity Prayer," original version quoted in Nancy S. Taylor, sermon "The Serenity Prayer," Old South Church, Boston, MA, July 1, 2007. Visit online at www.oldsouth.org/sermons/nst01jul07.htm.

31. William Lee Miller, "Beyond Serenity," *Boston Globe*, December 14, 2003. Visit online at www.boston.com/news/globe/ideas/articles/2003/12/14/beyond_serenity/.

32. "Rosemary McCombs-Maxey/Losemale Makomps Makse cvhocelkvtos: Justice Journey." *Finding Voice*, online at www.ucc.org/women/finding.html.

33. Mary Adamski, "Makahiki Allowed for Hawaii Inmates on Mainland," News Starbulletin.com, *Honolulu Star Bulletin*, February 8, 2005. Online at http://star bulletin.com/2005/02/08/news/story3.html.

34. See "The Reformation in England." Visit online at www.ucc.org/about-us/short-course/the-reformation-in-england.html.

35. William Davis, *Ancient Landmarks of Plymouth* (Boston: A. Williams & Company, 1883), 94. Also online at http://history-world.org/english_pilgrims.htm.

36. Quoted in Lowell H. Zuck, "Evangelical Pietism and Biblical Criticism: The Story of Karl Emil Otto," *Hidden Stories*, vol. 2, 78.

37. United Church of Christ Archives and Records, United Church of Christ, Cleveland OH. For more information, contact archivist and records manager at kellyb@ucc.org.

appendix

THE PREAMBLE OF THE CONSTITUTION OF THE UNITED CHURCH OF CHRIST AND THE STATEMENT OF FAITH

What are the sources from which we draw vital themes of our faith? We are shaped by historical creeds, centuries of prayerful reflection, and the lived experience of people putting their faith and witness on the line in challenging times.[1] The chapter "History Matters" describes many of those significant moments. Today, we often point to the following two statements.

THE PREAMBLE OF THE CONSTITUTION OF THE UNITED CHURCH OF CHRIST

Adopted in 1960, the Constitution of the UCC describes and regulates the work of General Synod as well as other agencies as the Covenanted Ministries of the national setting of the church. It also describes patterns of relationship for local churches, associations, conferences, and ministers to more effectively accomplish the work of the UCC. Paragraph 2 of the preamble offers a succinct theological and faith grounding for what follows.[2]

The United Church of Christ acknowledges as its sole Head, Jesus Christ, Son of God and Savior. It acknowledges as kindred in Christ all who share in this confession. It looks to the Word of God in the Scriptures, and to the presence and power of the Holy Spirit, to prosper its creative and redemptive work in the world. It claims as its own the faith of the historic Church expressed in the ancient creeds and reclaimed in the basic insights of the Protestant Reformers. It affirms the responsibility of the Church in each generation to make this faith its own in reality of worship, in honesty of thought and expression, and in purity of heart before God. In accordance with the teaching of our Lord and the practice prevailing among evangelical Christians, it recognizes two sacraments: Baptism and the Lord's Supper or Holy Communion.

UNITED CHURCH OF CHRIST STATEMENT OF FAITH

The original Statement of Faith was approved by the General Synod of the UCC in 1959. As chair of the commission that prepared the statement, Elmer J. F. Arndt explained the intent of the statement in this way: "The Statement of Faith is a testimony to 'the faith commonly held' in the United Church of Christ. It is not a 'test'; indeed, it is not a body of theological definitions. Rather it declares in words of our own time basic Christian and biblical affirmations and convictions."[3]

The following version in the form of a Doxology was affirmed by General Synod in 1981.

We believe in you, O God, Eternal Spirit,
God of our Savior Jesus Christ and our God,
and to your deeds we testify:
You call the worlds into being,
    create persons in your own image,
    and set before each one the ways of life and death.
You seek in holy love to save all people from aimlessness and sin.
You judge people and nations by your righteous will
declared through prophets and apostles.
In Jesus Christ, the man of Nazareth, our crucified and risen Savior,
    you have come to us
    and shared our common lot,
    conquering sin and death
    and reconciling the world to yourself.

You bestow upon us your Holy Spirit,
    creating and renewing the church of Jesus Christ,
    binding in covenant faithful people of all ages,
    tongues, and races.
You call us into your church
    to accept the cost and joy of discipleship,
    to be your servants in the service of others,
    to proclaim the gospel to all the world
    and resist the powers of evil,
    to share in Christ's baptism and eat at his table,
    to join him in his passion and victory.
You promise to all who trust you
    forgiveness of sins and fullness of grace,
    courage in the struggle for justice and peace,
    your presence in trial and rejoicing,
    and eternal life in your realm which has no end.
Blessing and honor, glory and power be unto you.
Amen.[4]

NOTES

1. For additional creeds, statements, and documents that shape the United Church of Christ, visit online www.ucc.org/beliefs/.

2. *The Constitution and Bylaws: United Church of Christ* (Cleveland: Executive Council for the United Church of Christ, 2000), 2.

3. Elmer J. F. Arndt, "Statement of Faith: Brief Introduction," *The Living Theological Heritage of the United Church of Christ*, vol. 7, eds. Frederick R. Trost and Barbara Brown Zikmund (Cleveland: Pilgrim Press, 2005), Doc. 4, 25.

4. For further information on the development and interpretation of the "Statement of Faith of the United Church of Christ" see, Roger L. Shinn, *Confessing Our Faith* (New York: Pilgrim Press, 1990).

Religion/Christianity/United Church of Christ (Congregational)

What Matters to You, Matters to Us
Engaging Six Vital Themes of Our Faith

Sidney D. Fowler

What Matters to You, Matters to Us provides essential reflections on core
themes of the United Church of Christ, while inviting new and long-standing
members alike to consider their own identity and faith formation.

Six central themes invite engagement:
1) We Are People of God's Extravagant Welcome
2) We Belong to Christ
3) We Are a People of Covenant, a United and Uniting Church
4) We Are One at Baptism and the Table
5) We Thank God by Working for a Just and Loving World
6) We Listen for the Still-speaking God

A seventh chapter offers historical examples. The United Church of Christ's
Statement of Faith and the Preamble to the Constitution are also included.

SIDNEY D. FOWLER is a consultant who assists congregations to become centers
of spiritual formation through worship, sacraments, prayer, education, the arts,
and spiritual discernment. Currently, he directs the lectionary project for the
Human Rights Campaign (HRC); is interim pastor of Hope United Church of
Christ, Alexandria, VA; and teaches with Shalem Institute for Spiritual Formation.
Fowler was the United Church of Christ's minister for worship, liturgy, and spiritual
formation for thirteen years. He earned his Ed.D. in religion and education from
Union Theological Seminary and Columbia University in the City of New York.

UNITED
CHURCH
PRESS®

$8.00 North America

ISBN 978-0-8298-1800-0

50800

9 780829 818000

unitedchurchpress.com
Cleveland, Ohio

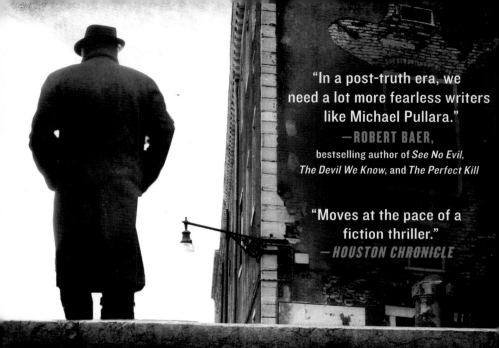

THE SPY WHO WAS
LEFT BEHIND

Russia, the United States, and the
True Story of the Betrayal and
Assassination of a CIA Agent

MICHAEL PULLARA